ISEHO MF

the competitor's

the

handbook

LESLEY BAYLEY

the
competitor's
handbook

WARD LOCK

A WARD LOCK BOOK

First published in the UK 1997
by Ward Lock
Wellington House
125 Strand
LONDON
WC2R 0BB

A Cassell Imprint

Distributed in the United States by
Sterling Publishing Co., Inc.
387 Park Avenue South, New York, NY 10016-8810

A British Library Cataloguing in Publication Data block for this book may be obtained from the British Library

ISBN 0 7063 7393 6

Computer make-up by Penny Mills, Wrentham, Suffolk
Printed and bound in Great Britain by The Bath Press

Contents

ONE

Why Compete?

Riding horses is a pleasurable pastime, giving people the chance to enjoy a relaxing time in the countryside and experience some of the sights and sounds of nature which might be missed when simply passing through by car. Riding out around the fields and lanes can produce many special moments, both in relation to the natural surroundings and, most importantly if you are a keen rider, in your developing partnership with your horse – so, with all this to be gained from simple hacking or leisure riding, why is it that some people aspire to competition?

Competitive riders may spend weeks, months, even years preparing for their chosen sport, laying out vast sums of money on training, travelling and competing. They will experience moments of great elation and, just as frequently, times of huge disappointment. What is it that keeps these people on their chosen path?

As you watch an event rider winning the world-famous Badminton Horse

A bold and confident jump over a corner – one of the thrills of competition. This rider has ridden her selected line very accurately and positively and her horse has responded with a neat jump.

Trials, a showjumper claiming the Hickstead Derby prize, or a dressage rider proudly riding in to represent their country, you can see immediately why all the effort has been worthwhile. Reaching the pinnacle of your sport provides a tremendous sense of achievement, and all the struggle along the way pales into insignificance: you have reached your goal, and shown everyone that you have the talent, determination and will to win.

Fine, you may say, that might apply to the top riders, but what about me, the ordinary horse owner? In fact, the pleasures – and pitfalls – of competing apply just as much to the ordinary rider as they do to those who have 'made it' and are known throughout the equestrian world. Never forget that at one time the likes of Mark Todd, Bruce Davidson, David O'Connor, John and Michael Whitaker, Greg Best, Conrad Homfeld, Nick Skelton, Tim Stockdale, Emile Faurie, Robert Dover, Laura Fry and Jennie Loriston-Clarke, now well known and respected, were once novice competitors too. In eventing, for example, Lucinda Green started off in Pony Club competitions on Be Fair, the horse that was to take her to the very top of the tree; Ginny Elliot visited Badminton as a young spectator and dreamed of competing there; and Mary King had several part-time jobs so that she could afford a horse to take to competitions.

Everyone, top riders included, starts off at the bottom of the competitive ladder, and how far up it you rise depends entirely on you. Having a good horse helps, and being able to afford expert tuition is certainly a bonus, but without the will to do well and the determination that keeps you going through the tough times, you will not realize your potential despite any material advantages.

Of course, there are as many reasons for competing as there are riders out there doing it. Perhaps you have only just thought about trying your hand at competition, so the idea of progressing through the levels has not entered your head – yet. On the other hand, you may have been inspired by a visit to a show or other event and be set on emulating your own particular hero or heroine. Some riders use competitions as a means of checking out their horse's training progress, while others compete purely to 'show off' and collect the trappings of success. Some people have a low-key attitude to competing at shows and take part purely for fun. Alternatively, you might just want to 'have a go' at a few competitions to see how you get on.

Whatever your reasons, if you approach the whole idea of competing properly you will be better prepared, your riding skills will improve, and the benefits of a positive attitude will also bring rewards in other aspects of your life.

IMPROVING YOUR RIDING

Deciding to compete and working towards a specific competition – whether it be your first-ever attempt at a dressage test or your fifty-first showjumping round – will concentrate your mind and efforts wonderfully. For example, simply practising the various movements required for a dressage test will require you to:

- Examine what is demanded by the test.
- Analyse each movement and the correct way to perform it.

Have a goal for each schooling session and bear in mind that you are meant to be enjoying yourself.

- Understand the aids for each movement.
- Work out what may go wrong and how to pre-empt or correct it.
- Practise movements until they are as good as you can possibly achieve.

In doing all this, your understanding of your horse's way of going and how you affect it will be increased, and your 'feel' for what is happening underneath you will develop steadily. By setting yourself goals and time limits, you create a structure within which to work and the impetus to keep going.

It is only by constantly stretching yourself that you will make progress: a rider may have 10 years' experience, but be no better than someone with just a year in the sport. Your attitude is extremely important. If you are content to sit back and never improve, that is fine (as long as your horse does not suffer from your lack of skill), but if you want to get the most out of your sport, to ride each horse to the best of its and your ability, and continually improve your skills, then working towards competitions will help. By aiming to compete you will have to:

- Analyse yourself and your performances.
- Criticize your riding *constructively*.
- Learn how to refine your aids.
- Get to know your horse, who is your partner in competition.
- Learn how to cope with setbacks and rebuild confidence.

All these will help you to increase your riding skills and develop a positive attitude towards your chosen sport.

REWARDS OF COMPETITION

Competing is challenging, stimulating and hard work. Even at the lowest levels, you will have to put yourself out; for example, as a basis for any competitive work you will need to get your horse fit, which often means getting up to ride when it is cold and pouring with rain.

But competing is also fun. In eventing and hunter trialling, there is the excitement of galloping across country and tackling fixed fences, knowing that you and your horse are well prepared. In showjumping, there is the satisfaction of working out a jump-off route which is tricky but which, if it pays off, will give you an unassailable lead. In endurance competitions, there is the tremendous achievement of riding a horse for mile upon mile over difficult terrain, and crossing the finish knowing that your mount is fit and well enough to be able to do the whole trip again. For the pure showing enthusiast, there is the thrill of showing off a horse to its best advantage under the scrutiny of an expert judge. In dressage, there is the wonderful feeling of lightness and power when you work a horse correctly, resulting in a test which is fluent and a joy to watch. Finally, whatever your chosen discipline, there is the satisfaction of a job well done, and of all the homework coming to fruition.

TYPES OF COMPETITION

Throughout the equestrian countries of the world there is a vast array of competitions taking place. Some are seasonal, while many take place all year round, if necessary moving indoors in winter. You can take your pick from showjumping, dressage, showing, driving, eventing, hunter trialling, western riding, side-saddle riding, endurance riding – you can try them all, several, or concentrate on just one. Many newcomers to competition have a go at several different types in order to decide which they like best; some people enjoy the challenges offered by the different sports and continue to participate in several disciplines, while others decide early on that one particular sport is for them and then stick with it.

Shows and events are organized by many different groups, associations and equestrian enterprises, and at levels ranging from local to international. The smaller shows will be advertised in local papers, on the noticeboards in saddlers and feed merchants, and in the national equestrian media. Riding schools often organize friendly novice shows, so check out these too.

Larger events are usually affiliated to the governing body of the particular discipline, with the various classes run under its rules, and may take place at a permanent venue. Breed societies, and associations for particular types of horse (such as piebalds and skewbalds, palominos, and the various classifications of show horses, cobs and ponies), also run shows for their members or hold classes at events run by other organizations.

At the back of the book you will find a Useful Addresses section listing organizations responsible for a wide range of competitive disciplines. Pony clubs and riding clubs organize shows for their members, rallies (mounted and dismounted), clinics, lectures, riding and stable management tests and more. Tuition is often provided at a greatly reduced rate, so it is well worth investigating the action in your area. If you are thinking of progressing beyond local shows and events, it is well worth contacting the relevant organizations. They will be able to provide you with details of the costs and benefits of membership, the structure of affiliated competitions, registration and grading of your horse, and more.

USING THIS BOOK

Whether you are new to competition, returning to it after a long break, or are hoping to re-establish your confidence, overcome fear or simply have a good time, this book is designed to help you

achieve your aims. It is intended to be used as a working reference, for you to turn to time and again, whatever your chosen discipline. In addition to the detailed text and informative diagrams and photographs, each chapter also features at-a-glance summaries, action points, checklists and tips to help you find the information you need quickly and easily.

You may also find it useful to jot down words or phrases which have particular relevance for you, to serve as 'pick-me-ups' when the going gets tough. A personal favourite, and one which is particularly appropriate in the context of competing with horses, is:

Failure is not falling down, failure is failing to get up again once you are down.

You will make mistakes – everyone does – but by learning from them, both

When you meet resistance, you first need to analyse the reasons behind it and then consider how you can overcome the difficulty.

your riding and your horse will improve. It is only by getting things wrong that you can learn how to cope with problems. The worst thing you can do is to close your mind and become entrenched in one way of doing things: in the horse world, you will discover that there are many different ways of attacking the same problem. Moreover, each horse, and rider, is an individual combination, and what works for one combination may prove to be disastrous for another. You will come across conflicts of opinion, but do try to keep an open mind: be receptive to different ideas, question the thinking behind them, then discard what will not work for you and your horse, and adopt and adapt anything which might help you.

This book is one framework to assist you. Don't just read it – *use* it, and give yourself a leg up on to the first rung of the competitive ladder.

ACTION POINT

Find out where local shows and events are held and visit them as a spectator to see which types of activity interest you.

SUMMARY

■ While leisure riding is enjoyable, competing adds a new dimension to your hobby.

■ Preparing for competition helps you to clarify your goals, so that the whole process of improving your skills is more structured.

■ Your riding progress is limited mainly by your mental attitude.

■ There is a wide choice of competitive activities, with something to suit all horses and riders.

■ Use this book as a working reference manual to help you prepare for and enjoy competitions.

TWO

Preparation – Riding

Before you launch yourself into the competitive fray, take a little time to decide where your talents lie. The chances are that you will find it difficult to make a realistic assessment of your riding ability. People tend to fall into two categories: those who dramatically over-estimate their skills, and those who have a much more self-effacing attitude. Both groups need help!

SELF ASSESSMENT

If you have a regular instructor, ask him or her to give you an honest opinion on your strengths and weaknesses. In addition to this, or if you do not have an instructor, try this self-assessment exercise. Without thinking about the following questions for too long, write down your 'gut' reactions:

1 What do you enjoy most about riding?

2 What do you really dislike about riding?

3 Which equestrian sport appeals to you most? Why?

4 Which equestrian sport appeals to you least? Why?

5 Which famous event or show would you like to ride at? If none, state 'none'.

6 Would you say 'I wish I was a three-day eventer/showjumper etc' or 'I want to be a three-day eventer/showjumper etc'?

7 Imagine yourself riding at a show – is your performance good, bad or indifferent?

8 You have a choice between going out with friends for the evening or taking your horse to a training session. Which do you prefer to do? Which will you do?

9 On a scale of 1 (low) to 10 (high), how would you rate your dedication/commitment to horses?

Armed with your honest answers, check out the following points about each question:

1 If you are going to be successful at anything you really do have to enjoy doing it! This may sound obvious, but it is amazing how many people neglect to consider this aspect – just think of all the people you know who have started out on exercise programmes but soon lapsed. There are bound to be times when you

Don't cut yourself off when preparing for competitions – you and your horse will enjoy the company of others and a constructive friend can help with your preparation.

would prefer to go straight home instead of heading for the stables; this is only natural, and it is the fact that deep down you enjoy what you are doing that will give you the incentive to get out and ride your horse in the cold and wet, when you are feeling below par, and so on.

If jumping is what you really enjoy, there is no need to force yourself to enter show classes or dressage competitions (unless, of course, you want to event, in which case the dressage phase becomes very important). Do remember, though, that you will have to put some work into schooling your horse on the flat in order to achieve results in the jumping arena. I know of one rider who absolutely hates flatwork and is fanatical about jumping. For years she has struggled to get any kind of results in showjumping and almost gave up because her horse was so uncooperative. Recently, circumstances forced her to work on simple flatwork exercises, and this year has seen her being placed in most of the jumping classes she has entered. Her success is the result of her horse's increased obedience and suppleness, achieved through the discipline of flatwork.

2 It is not unusual for people to dislike something about riding – for many, the boredom of walking their horse for the initial weeks of a fitness programme falls into this category. It is fine to dislike some aspect or other, provided that in doing so you do not neglect this facet of your riding (as the example in 1 above proved, where neglecting flatwork hampered that particular horse and rider's progress).

First admit that you dislike something and then work out ways in which to make this particular task more pleasant. For example, if you too dislike flatwork, seek the help of a good instructor who will give you plenty of exercises to work on. You can then use these in your sessions at home so that your schooling is more imaginative and therefore less boring. You can also work on 'schooling' exercises while out hacking, or ride with a friend so that you can comment (constructively and tactfully) on each other's efforts.

If you dislike caring for horses, as opposed to riding, then you ought to think seriously about whether you should be competing. Success in the ring depends not only on your riding on the day but also on your preparation, and your feeding and fitness programmes. If you cannot be bothered to put in the work here then you will not achieve your goals, unless of course you can afford to pay someone else to do all the preparatory work, but this is certainly a far less rewarding route.

3 Just why do you like your favourite equestrian sport? Is it the glamour of the occasion? Remember that before you get close to the top venues there will be many years of small shows and events to get through. Do you have the sticking power to cope with all the 'small stuff' first? If not, perhaps you do not really want to compete but are better suited to being a spectator. Only you can decide, and you will have to be honest with yourself.

If eventing is your favourite sport, are you as enthusiastic about the dressage and showjumping phases as about the cross country? If it is purely the cross country riding which excites you, then hunter trialling would fulfil your needs without the additional expense and work involved in developing your dressage and showjumping skills.

Don't forget that all sports have their various levels, so if you fancy showjumping but are scared at the sight of the Hickstead fences, you can still enjoy the smaller classes at local shows. Who knows – you may change your view of the top-class events once your skills develop and your confidence increases.

4   While there is little point in competing in a class which you do not enjoy, you may find that your horse is best suited to the one equestrian discipline that you dislike. Are you prepared to sell him, or buy an additional horse, so that you can enjoy your chosen sport? Could you afford to do this? If not, can you enjoy the challenge of producing your horse to the best of his ability in his discipline?

Can you pinpoint why you dislike a particular activity? If your dislike is based on a lack of knowledge or experience of the sport, then do open your mind and have a go before condemning it as unsuitable for you.

5   We all have dreams, and what may seem out of reach now may not be so far off once you have spent a couple of years developing your skills. There is a saying that if you can imagine it, you can achieve it, and if you can dream it, you can become it. A positive mental attitude will help you achieve a great deal, so do believe in yourself. Even if you do not make it all the way, you will have travelled very much further down the road to success than those who always doubt themselves.

6   Wishing you were a better rider or could tackle fences with the confidence and skill of Mark Todd is not enough. People who only 'wish' rather than 'want' tend to stay in the comfortable, less demanding world of daydreams. Saying that you want to be a showjumper, eventer or whatever is a statement of intent, which you then reinforce by doing something about it. People who want rather than wish have their action plans – the steps towards achieving their goals.

While it is unrealistic and demoralizing to set yourself ridiculous goals, you must set yourself targets which will stretch you and provide a sense of satisfaction when you reach them. Break down your long-term objective into manageable chunks: no-one expects you to go from being a newcomer to riding to becoming a member of the local riding club eventing team in three months! Your goals should be split into short, medium and long term, with time scales and points of reference along the way.

For example, your long-term aim may be to become a member of the riding club eventing team in two years' time. Your medium-term goal could then be to compete regularly and successfully in dressage, showjumping and cross country classes in a year's time. Your short-term goals will be to improve your horse's schooling so that his dressage performances progress consistently, and to work on gymnastic jumping and cross country schooling.

These are broad statements of your goals and time scales: now you need to break down the short-term goals even further and decide on your points of reference. For example, some people are pleased if they get round a showjumping

Riding in a competition can be a nerve-racking experience. This rider is gripping up with her legs as she anxiously tries to get her pony going forwards.

course with two refusals, but if you are aiming to become a team member, consistent clear rounds will be required. To break down your short-term programme, you will need to look at your own and your horse's experience so far and decide what is needed to reach your medium-term goal. For example, your weakness may be showjumping, so more attention will be needed here.

7 The importance of mental attitude has already been stressed, and one of the 'tricks' that successful riders use is mental rehearsal. This has been applied by athletes in many different sports and really does work. You simply rehearse your dressage test, showjumping round or individual show in your head, as if you are playing a video to yourself. You have control, so you can have yourself sailing over fences, producing fluid dressage movements, winning the class and so on. You will also be able to rehearse all the feelings you get and corrections you need to make as the round or test progresses. All this reinforces your positive attitude and allows you to practise the skills you need subconsciously, in order to achieve a successful result.

Research has shown that people who mentally rehearse their performances in this positive way do increase their skill level. On the other hand, if you allow yourself to rehearse failure then the chances are that failure will occur. You can train yourself to be a loser – but it is just as effective and much more fun training yourself to be a winner!

8 Being successful at anything takes an incredible amount of effort, but all work and no play can make you miserable. If you are working towards goals and have action plans, you will know whether you are falling behind your schedule or are achieving your target. If the latter is the case, then you can enjoy a social outing without feeling guilty. While top-level success comes from being extremely focused on your objectives, it is important that you keep a balance in your life.

9 Dedication and commitment are required in vast measure in order to take part in equestrian competition. Just keeping horses, let alone competing, is a huge drain on your money and time. Your horse relies on you for every aspect of his well being: it is your responsibility to feed and water him, so that all his nutritional needs are fulfilled; to recognize when all is not well and seek veterinary attention as required; to keep him exercised; to ensure that his stable and field meet all his needs; and to keep him happy mentally and emotionally as well as physically.

ASSESSING YOUR HORSE

Alongside your own attitude to horse ownership and competing, your horse's abilities and inclinations will also make a crucial contribution to any success – or otherwise – you may achieve.

While correct training can develop a horse's talents, it is far more pleasurable to work with a tractable horse than it is to deal with a resistant, argumentative animal. If you want to enjoy jumping cross country fences, for example, choose a bold, responsive animal rather than one which is unwilling to gallop and backs off solid obstacles. For the show ring, you will start with a distinct advantage if your horse has a lot of natural presence and will 'play' to the audience, instead of having to be cajoled into showing off his attributes. In endurance, a horse with natural ability to cover the ground, trotting and cantering effortlessly and then being very relaxed at vet checks, will be a good prospect, while an excitable, flighty one will waste considerable energy and also time.

You will need to assess your horse's abilities, preferably with the help of an experienced horseman/woman or instructor who can give an unbiased opinion on the horse's current experience, future potential and possible problem areas.

Consider factors such as your horse's previous experiences (or lack of them). For example, is he wary of jumping into water through inexperience or due to a previous bad experience in water? Is he currently hampered as a showjumper because he is overweight and unfit? Will your horse's age hamper your competitive plans? I did hear of someone who wanted to novice event a 19-year-old horse that was obese, stiff and had never competed. Now that *is* starting off with a disadvantage!

Whatever discipline you intend to pursue, your horse's conformation has to be considered. While the perfect horse does not exist, the better your horse's conformation the more likely it is that he will be able to withstand the demands of work and competition. Some conformation defects will make a horse more prone to injury – for example, horses who are 'back at the knee' are more susceptible to tendon trouble.

While your horse's skeletal structure cannot be changed, his muscular development can be affected by training.

A progressive schooling programme can also, for example, improve a horse's technique over fences, but it will have only a limited effect if his attitude and temperament are poor. Most horses are genuine, willing-to-please types, but if you do have an ungenuine horse your success will always be limited.

FOOD FOR THOUGHT

■ How do you deal with problems? Do you see them as major catastrophes or as opportunities for learning? If you always regard them as your chance to fail, it is time to rethink your attitude! Stop training yourself to be a loser and start improving your self-image. Banish the word 'problem' from your vocabulary and substitute 'opportunity'. There is something to be gained from every situation – you just need to learn how to recognize the lesson being offered.

■ What is your reaction to change? If you do not like it, then the chances are that you will progress much more slowly, in any aspect of life, than someone who sees change as a chance for personal growth and development. Remember that riding is a life-long process – this is one art which cannot be mastered in a short time.

■ Do not let your fears get the better of you: the anticipation is often more frightening than

There will be times when everything is going right – and times when your riding seems to be standing still. This is when a positive mental attitude will keep you plugging on.

the event itself. Recognize what is causing you anxiety and face up to it, and you will then be able to move on.

■ Is your approach to riding and horse care efficent or effective? Efficiency is doing something well, effectiveness is doing the right thing well.

■ Remember: goals fulfil *your* wishes, not someone else's.

ASSESSMENT CHECKLIST

Consider the following points when assessing your horse:

■ Conformation

■ Breeding

■ Paces

■ Aptitude for the job

■ Temperament

PARTNERSHIP

You must really like your horse if you and he are to go places together. You can be competitive and compassionate: if you like your horse, you will be able to apply all the training and discipline but with compassion. Top event rider Robert Lemieux feels that the relationship between horse and rider is extremely important: 'I have to be in love with the horse I ride.'

FORMULATING AN ACTION PLAN

Armed with a realistic assessment of your horse's experience and abilities, together with some idea of your own talents and weaknesses, you can now start to formulate your competition action plan. To show how this might work, let us take the example of a rider planning to go eventing with her eight-year-old horse. The horse completed some pre-novice events with his previous owner, while the rider has competed at riding club level for a number of years. She has bought the horse in autumn and is planning to start competing the following spring. Looking at this situation, the rider decides to work on the following areas:

Partnership As the combination of horse and rider is new, it will take some time for each party to develop trust and confidence in the other. Only by riding the horse and spending time grooming, feeding and generally looking after him will the rider get to know her horse. The first priority is therefore to sort out a workable daily plan, which will enable the rider to look after her horse properly at the same time as fulfilling her other obligations to work and family.

In doing this, our rider finds that she cannot really give the horse the work he needs, so she must find someone else who can help with the exercising.

Dressage Both horse and rider enjoy dressage, and the rider sees this phase as a chance to start an event with a good mark. However, she knows that it is only by constant practice, and by setting goals for each schooling session (which may need to be flexible, depending on how the horse is going), that she will be able to improve her horse's suppleness, obedience and ultimate performance in the dressage ring.

To meet these requirements, our rider plans to include three sessions of dressage in the weekly riding programme, and determines to find a good instructor whom she can visit twice a month in order to keep both herself and her horse on the right track.

Remember to budget for lessons – whatever discipline you are planning to compete in, your horse will be more supple, obedient and responsive if he is worked regularly on the flat.

Showjumping Although the horse has talent here, this is our rider's weakest phase. Her first task is therefore to find someone who can help, preferably on a weekly basis. She also determines to get out and compete as often as possible throughout the winter on the indoor showjumping circuit.

Cross country This is the phase that our rider enjoys most, but her horse is relatively inexperienced. She therefore decides to seek out hunter trials and cross country competitions so that the combination can gain experience together. She also plans to take the horse hunting or draghunting on several occasions to get him thinking forward and enjoying himself across country.

General care Our rider is aware that grooming, feeding and fitness are essential to the well being of the competition horse. As she has previously kept the horse in full livery but is now entirely responsible for her horse's welfare herself, she makes use of the free nutritional advice service offered by feed companies to compile a feeding programme. Closely linked to this is the horse's fitness programme, and here the rider consults books, magazines and riding club friends for all possible information on getting her horse fit for competition. She also determines to use the winter to practise her plaiting and trimming skills, so that she can turn her horse out properly for the spring competitions.

Time schedules The rider uses an old horse trials schedule to plan out roughly where she wants to compete and when. Working back from this, she can then sort out the fitness programme and plan all the little competitions she wants to enter in the lead-up to her major events.

From this example, you will see that a great deal of forward thinking and planning is required if you intend to compete successfully. Although we have used eventing as our illustration, a small showjumping class at the local gymkhana, say, will need a similar approach, although the details requiring your attention will be different. For instance, first-time competitors will have to consider such points as whether or not they have the correct clothes, and if not, whether they will be able to buy or borrow them; how they are going to transport the horse to the show; how they can fit in some lessons to ensure that they and their horse are well used to jumping courses before the show itself, and so on. Whatever the level at which you are riding, there is a degree of planning involved in competing, and ensuring that you carry out this preparation properly will result in a much better experience for you at the competition itself.

IMPORTANCE OF HOMEWORK

Whether you are planning to go showjumping or eventing, take part in dressage competitions or working hunter classes, or try 175-km (100-mile) endurance rides, it is important that you school your horse on the flat. The horse naturally carries the bulk of his weight on his forehand, and during training we try to redistribute it so that he carries more of it on his hindquarters and lightens his forehand. By doing this, the horse is able to carry himself and his rider more effectively and efficiently, and his working life, whether in dressage, endurance or jumping, will be less stressful and hopefully longer as his body is being used

ACTION PLAN CHECKLIST

■ Decide on the event and classes you wish to enter.

■ Know exactly what is required of you and your horse.

■ Work out an action plan and time schedule, so that you and your horse are fully prepared.

■ Allow time in your programme for things to go wrong.

■ Remember to budget for lessons, transport to these and to the show, entry fees and so on. If you do this right at the start you will know whether you can actually afford to fulfil your ambitions or need to rethink; for instance, you could concentrate on just one discipline this year instead of trying to compete in both dressage and showjumping.

to its optimum capability. Working your horse on the flat also helps to increase his obedience, athletic ability and suppleness – both longitudinally (from front to rear) and laterally (from side to side), and will improve his rhythm and balance.

There has to be a sequence of work in training: too often riders concentrate on forcing the horse into an 'outline', by which they often mean pulling in the horse's head while the hindquarters are left trailing behind, thus making it difficult for him to use himself properly and impossible for him to work in the 'outline' for which they are supposedly aiming. In very basic terms, a horse is working in a correct outline when his hindquarters are engaged, his back is raised and round, and his head is carried near to the vertical. He moves forward calmly and freely, with straightness and rhythm, and without resistance. The horse's level of training and, to some extent, his conformation, will affect his outline. When in a correct outline the horse is using himself efficiently, which is desirable.

Structure your horse's schooling programme so that you first achieve obedience from him. Then think about him going forwards, at a speed which you, not he, dictates. Once these two prerequisites are established, rhythm and outline will follow in time.

REMEMBER

Each time you school your horse you should create a situation in which he can learn something.

ENDURANCE AND OUTLINE

Endurance horses are not ridden in an outline as generally understood. They are, however, ridden forwards calmly with the hindquarters engaged, but on a longer rein, with the head and neck freer than one would see, for example, in a dressage horse. As the endurance horse is crossing varied terrain at speed, he needs the freedom of his head and neck to help balance himself.

Checking your riding

How your horse goes under saddle is directly related to your riding position and use of the aids. So, before you start working on your horse, think about yourself.

Before you even mount, it is worth taking a few minutes to get yourself warmed up, loosened off and ready to ride – as soon as you mount you start to warm up your horse, so it is logical to have a warming-up procedure for yourself as well.

Once on board, run through your position:

- Is your upper body tall, or have you slumped your shoulders and collapsed your diaphragm?
- Is your head on top of your shoulders, or are you tipping it forwards or back?
- Are you sitting centrally, with your weight evenly distributed?
- Is there a straight line from your ear

down through your shoulder, hip and heel?

- Is there a straight line from your elbow, through your hand and along the rein to the bit? If you bring your hands down you will be bringing the bit down on to the bars of the horse's mouth.
- Are you relaxed?
- Is your lower leg on the girth?
- Is your toe to the front?
- Once you move off, can you maintain a good position?
- Are you aware if your leg is slipping back or your hands are becoming unlevel?

And so on. Think about your position and make adjustments to it as and when required. You should always be aiming at the ideal, for the riding position has evolved because it enables the horse to carry his rider in the most efficient and effective way. Be aware at all times. For instance, when executing turns and circles:

- Are you aware of where your inside leg and rein are positioned?
- What is happening to your outside leg and hand?
- Are your shoulders following the line of your horse's shoulders?
- In trot, are you on the correct diagonal? Are you rising too high and making too much effort? Are you banging back down into the saddle instead of sitting softly?
- In canter, do you tip forward during transitions? Does your lower leg move around? Is your upper body still or rocking?

Keep all these questions in mind, so that when you ride you can correct yourself –

TIP

As your horse goes into canter his inside shoulder will elevate, so do not make things more difficult for him by looking down at his shoulder during the transition.

---

this is especially useful when you have to work alone for long periods. If you do not make the effort to improve your riding, you will soon fall into bad habits.

By thinking about your riding in this way and asking yourself questions, you will give yourself guidelines as to where you need to improve. You can then set yourself goals for each schooling session – and knowing what you intend to do means that you can prepare beforehand. For example, even if you think you know the aids for leg yielding, it is as well to read up on the movement in advance, so that when you try it in practice you are perfectly clear about what you and the horse should be doing.

TIP

Use photographs and videos of yourself riding as tools to help you develop your skills.

Organizing your schooling

As already explained, the key to any competitive success lies in your horse's basic flatwork. If the foundations are good and the horse is responsive to the aids, supple, obedient, in balance and works in a good rhythm, then he will find more complicated work such as jumping

If you can have your schooling sessions photographed or videotaped you will learn a great deal from this visual record.

grids of fences and negotiating cross country obstacles much easier. In addition, working your horse correctly on the flat will help to develop the correct muscles to enable him to carry both himself and you more efficiently. Just like riders, some horses enjoy working on the flat more than others, but whatever your or your horse's preferences, it is vital that you do pay attention to this important aspect of his education.

A little practice every day, or several sessions a week, is more beneficial that one major hit each week. Train yourself to ride accurate movements; for instance, when executing transitions, decide that you will walk at C or halt at X and do it, spot on! You can also incorporate some schooling into hacks, for instance using shoulder-in to go past roadside hazards, practising leg yielding along empty tracks, and utilizing turn on the forehand for opening gates.

It helps to have schooling goals to aim for in each of your work sessions, but in order to do this you must first assess your horse's needs (and your own). You will find that the help of an instructor is invaluable here, since someone 'on the ground' is in a better position to judge whether hiccups are caused by rider error, equine bolshiness or a lack of understanding on the part of the horse.

Making your assessment

In assessing your horse, treat him as if he is a total stranger to you. When you get on and work him you will need the answers to the following questions:

- Does he go forward from your leg aids?
- Does he stop when you ask?
- Can you steer him easily?

From this basic information you can move on to further questions, for example:

- Does the horse need to be encouraged forwards more, or should he be slowed down?
- Are his paces rhythmical or are they erratic?
- Does he feel balanced all the time, or just occasionally? What affects his balance?
- Does he understand your aids?
- Which is his better rein? How bad is the other rein? Does this relate at all to the way you are riding him?

There are lots of ways in which a horse can evade your requests, for example by going much faster and running along on his forehand; dropping behind the bit and aids; snatching the reins out of your hands; falling out through his shoulder; refusing to go forwards – each horse has his own party trick, which he is normally quite happy to use unless the rider says otherwise!

So, you will need to discover the answers to the following set of questions as well:

- What evasions does the horse use?
- What can you do to correct this?
- How will he react if you insist that he does as you ask?
- Can you cope with his reaction?

Finding solutions

Once you have made your assessment of your horse, and considered how your riding may be contributing to or emphasizing a problem, you will need to decide on the best course of action.

The speed merchant Let's assume that your horse is extremely forward going, using speed as an evasion. Instead of executing smooth transitions or cantering a circle calmly, you find yourself hurtling everywhere at breakneck speed. Firstly, you need to establish why your horse is like this. Pain is often a contributory factor, so:

● Check your horse's tack for fit.
● Check his teeth.
● Seek the help of your vet if necessary in order to determine if there are any physical causes for the behaviour (many horses suffer from pain or discomfort in the neck or back).

If physical causes are found, they must be treated and a programme of reschooling undertaken to show the horse that it is now okay to slow down – often the memory of pain stays with the animal even though the pain itself has been removed.

Endless patience will now be required to work the horse through transitions and exercises like circles, serpentines and loops at walk and trot, using halts and canter where appropriate. A little work each day will pay off. Riding over poles on the ground also adds interest – you could make up a labyrinth of poles through which the horse has to walk, stop, turn, walk on, and so on.

As the rider, you must remember to make use of your seat and weight aids to help steady the horse. If he tries to rush, bring him quietly back to walk and repeat the exercise. Eventually he will start to calm down. You must also remember to use your leg aids: with a lively horse it is tempting to keep your legs off his sides,

If your horse starts to misbehave, first check that the difficulty is not being caused by a physical problem.

but he must be taught gradually to accept the presence and use of the rider's legs.

The lazy horse   You may have the opposite problem of the horse being slow to respond to your leg. Starting in halt, ask your horse to move off by closing your legs around his sides and easing the rein slightly – you do not want him to move off and be rewarded by a jab in the mouth owing to inflexible, set hands on your part. If he does not respond, ask again, using a stronger leg aid. Should the horse still not respond, you must ask again, but back up your leg aid with a flick from your schooling whip (take care not to pull back on the rein as you use it). This should galvanize your horse.

You now need to practise halt-to-walk transitions so that your horse learns to respond to a *light* aid. There is no point in applying stronger and stronger aids, as the horse's sides will simply become 'deadened' and riding him will be even harder work for you.

When your horse is going forwards from halt to walk from a light aid, you can try walk-to-trot transitions. If he does not respond immediately, remind him by using the schooling whip as a back-up to the leg aid.

You must always be consistent in the way you ride your horse and in what you demand from him. There is nothing to be gained by insisting on an immediate response to the aids in the school and then letting him get away with a sloppy response out hacking.

If you are at all uncertain about how to cope with a particular problem, or if you feel you cannot cope, do ask an instructor to help as soon as possible. Trying to soldier on without assistance usually costs more in time, money and effort in the long run.

Some schooling exercises

At the start of a schooling session, always warm up and loosen your horse before asking him to perform any real work. Spend 10–15 minutes working initially in walk on a loose rein, on both reins, asking the horse to move away from your leg and perform walk-to-halt transitions. Then move on to some trot and canter work, again on both reins but without trying to make him work in an outline.

When you start to work the horse, again remember to ride on both reins to prevent

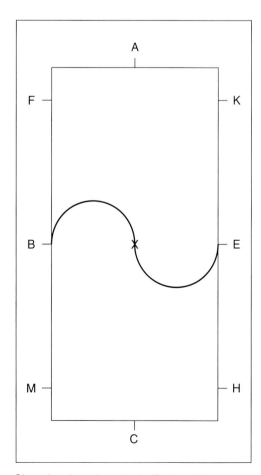

Changing the rein using half 10m circles.

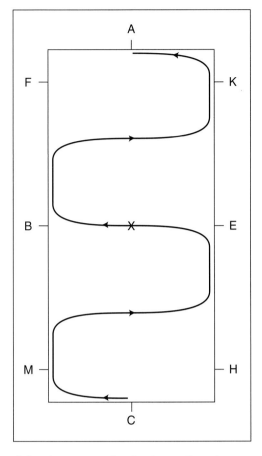

A four-loop serpentine to change the rein.

Changing the rein across the long diagonal.

or counteract one-sidedness. Frequent changes of rein make the work more interesting for both you and the horse, and there are many ways in which this can be done in order to introduce some variety:

- Half 10m circle right, for example from F on to the centre line, then down the centre line to X and then a half 10m circle left to E.
- Half 20m circle from A to X, then half 20m circle from X to C.
- Half 15m circle left or half 10m circle left, for example from K, then incline back to the track at H.

- Half 10m circle left at E to X, then half 10m circle right from X to B.
- Four-loop serpentine from A or C.
- Using the long or short diagonals.

Use 20m circles to improve the horse's lateral flexion and enable you to learn about co-ordinating your aids to produce a consistent bend from the horse. In order to ride accurate circles, remember to look far enough ahead throughout the exercise. You can combine 20m circles and work on figures-of-eight with simple changes of rein. Spiralling in and out of 20m circles is also useful and helps to get

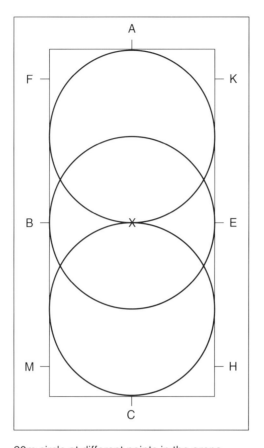

20m circle at different points in the arena.

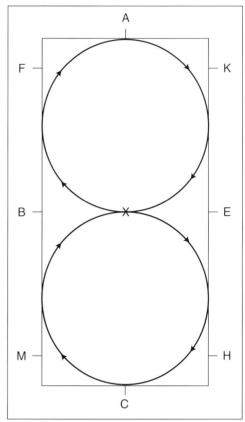

A figure-of-eight consisting of two 20m circles.

the horse listening to the rider's leg. Smaller circles may be used to improve the balance of both horse and rider and

to build on the suppleness of the horse. Serpentines encourage the horse to soften to your inside leg, while you will learn to

SCHOOLING TIPS

■ Work in a marked area so that you can assess your accuracy, for example when performing a 20m circle.

■ Know what you are trying to achieve, the aids for each particular movement or exercise, which pace it is best executed in and so on.

■ Write down your schooling goals, even to the point of noting the aids for a particular movement when you are learning something new. This will help to crystallize everything in your mind and will give you something against which to measure your performance afterwards.

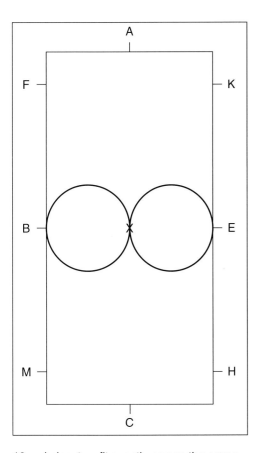

10m circles: two fit exactly across the arena.

obtain the correct bend and use your weight effectively.

Transitions are useful in getting the

INCREASING YOUR AWARENESS

You can increase your awareness of your horse's movement by saying 'now, now' as the horse's inside hind-leg comes underneath him on a circle.

Evenness of stride is a great help to a horse whether it is jumping or working on the flat, so train yourself to become more aware of your horse's stride using the following exercises:

- Place two white poles on the centre line of your school, 18m (20yd) apart. Work through them, counting the strides. Now try to decrease the number of strides you take between the poles. You must keep the strides even. Now increase the number of strides taken between the poles. You can do this same exercise between two points on the long side of the school.

- To improve your sense of rhythm and balance, ask your horse to trot on and then hold the rise position for three or four strides, sit for a designated number of strides, rise again, and so on. This exercise can also be done in canter, standing for six strides, then sitting for six.

horse to listen to you and are the way to work towards engaging his hindquarters. In order to achieve good transitions, always remember that the quality of a transition will be affected by the quality of the pace preceding it.

TIP

Can you tell if your horse is going forwards sufficiently? One way to determine whether or not the horse is walking for himself is to ask yourself 'Will the next stride be a walk stride (if walking) or a stop stride?' If it feels as though the horse is about to grind to a halt, then you need to wake him up and insist that he walks on smartly.

COMPETITION RIDING – A REAL-LIFE EXAMPLE

Now that we have discussed assessing both yourself and your horse, formulating an action plan, and the importance of flatwork in preparing your horse for any type of competition, let's take the real-life example of a horse and rider who are a relatively new partnership and have been working towards their first one-day event along the lines discussed in this chapter. The event consists of a novice horse-trials dressage test, a 0.85m (2ft 9in) show-jumping course and a 0.92m (3ft) cross country course.

Prior to the event, the rider had several jumping lessons with a good instructor and was tackling showjumping courses considerably bigger than she was going to meet on the day. Poor weather conditions meant that she and her horse had had very little cross country experience together, although the horse had successfully completed larger cross country courses with its previous owner. The new partnership had managed to fit in a few dressage lessons, and this was the phase the rider was least worried about. So, how did our rider get on at her first event?

Dressage

Working in In the dressage warm-up area the horse went very well, being forward going and attentive, and working in a nice outline with good rhythm. The only problem to crop up was a tendency to strike off on the incorrect canter lead on the right rein.

The test As this was the combination's first test together, the rider was careful to ride the horse around the outside of the dressage arena so that he could see the white marker boards and get any objections over with outside the arena. The horse ignored the boards, but on entering the arena decided to take exception to them, moving away from the outside track and ignoring the rider's pleas to move in a straight line. In addition, the horses in the adjoining arenas suddenly became very interesting!

The submissive horse from the warm-up area had turned into a lit-up animal with its head in the air, who felt to the rider as if he were about to charge off into the distance. As the horse was not concentrating, the canter strike-off on the right rein was incorrect and it took several strides for the rider to bring her argumentative horse back to trot in order to correct the mistake. However, the second canter was better, and finally, as the test was about to finish, the horse started to pay attention.

What the judges said Hurried and unbalanced from the horse, who also showed disobedience to the aids at times. Well ridden by the rider.

Showjumping

Working in The horse jumped beautifully over the practice fences, with the rider doing everything properly. They started off over a cross pole, moved on to an upright and then took on a spread. The rider then made use of the two practice jumps to create some flowing jumping and riding on.

In the ring Despite being very forward going in the collecting ring, once inside the arena the horse was transformed. The first few fences were just about passable, but

Winning a class – the result of your homework!

Working on a long, loose rein does not require the horse to activate his hindquarters. As the horse naturally carries 60 per cent of his weight on his forehand, the object of your schooling is to encourage him to transfer some of that weight on to his hindquarters so that he becomes lighter in front.

The rider is allowing her horse to fall on the forehand. The horse is not together and his hindquarters are trailing.

Result: the downward transition is also 'downhill', with the horse again falling on the forehand.

This horse has a long-striding, active trot even though he is not being asked to come into an outline and really use himself.

Here the rider has taken more of a contact and is asking the horse to come rounder, with the result that the trot is more active.

Look at the difference when the rider drops the contact – the horse has lost all activity in the trot.

Lungeing using two lines helps you to control the horse's quarters and ensures that the horse uses himself actively.

Working on circles, the rider must maintain just enough bend throughout the horse's body. Too much inside rein results in too much bend in the neck; giving away the outside rein allows the horse to fall out through his shoulder. The rider's outside leg helps prevent the horse's quarters swinging out, and the inside leg maintains the impulsion.

Cantering uphill as part of a horse's fitness programme. The initial foundations of plenty of slow, steady work are essential before the horse is moved on to more strenuous work.

A stencil can be used for making quarter marks when presenting your horse for the show ring.

A show class for piebalds and skewbalds. Many events run such classes, as coloured horses and ponies have become increasingly popular.

FAR LEFT *If your show class requires the judge to ride, do make sure that your horse is used to strangers riding him.*

LEFT *Some show classes require the horse to stand in line for a considerable time, and it is more pleasant for all concerned if he is taught to stand attentively but quietly.*

BELOW *Resistance will go against your horse in a show class, as the ride he gives is part of the overall mark.*

*If you are required
to trot up your
horse in hand,
practise this at
home so that your
performance in the
ring is impressive.*

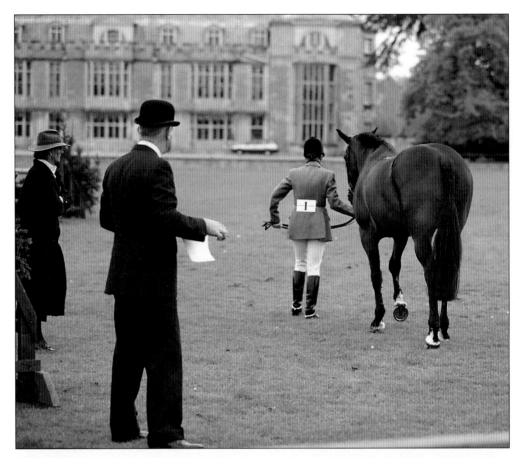

*A show horse
which has been
stripped and stood
up for the judge to
view.*

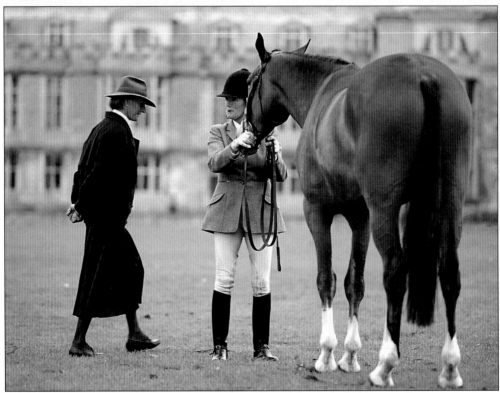

OPPOSITE *A typical
fence in a working
hunter class.*

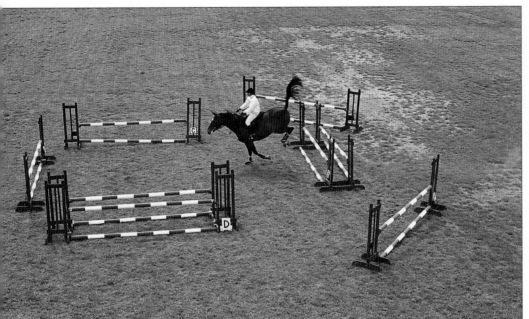

LEFT *Make use of gridwork exercises at home to increase your horse's suppleness, agility and obedience, and sharpen up your own reactions.*

BELOW *This rider is already looking for the next fence and is ready to turn – if you want to be successful in a jump-off situation you must practise turning and taking strides out. This is more effective than trying simply to go fast, which will inevitably encourage your horse to jump flat and knock down fences.*

OPPOSITE *You should be confident and competent when jumping at home before you venture out to a show. Initially, enter classes which are below the height you are jumping at home – then you can compete knowing that everything is well within your and your horse's capabilities.*

No matter how small the fence you still need to be a determined rider, fully committed to getting over it.

Warm up adequately, but do not leave your best jumps in the practice ring.

Playing in water with a friend – a good way to introduce horses to water and ensure that such obstacles present little problem to cross country or endurance horses.

Jumping down into water. You need sufficient impulsion but not too much boldness otherwise the drag of the water could result in the horse losing his footing. The rider must also be in balance: if you get too far forward you may go over the top if the horse pecks. You should be ready to ride the next stride, as this rider demonstrates.

A bold leap up a step – but the rider is ready, maintaining a good contact and using her legs to ensure that the horse still has the impulsion for the next step or obstacle.

You need to be ready for the unexpected. This horse has come up a slope to jump the log on the left-hand side of the picture – just look at the activity of his hindquarters.

Jumping ditches: the rider is looking up and away. Do not let your eyes be drawn to the bottom of the ditch, or you will inevitably end up stopping – or falling in!

A good consistent pace and rhythm make for a better cross country ride.

The day before a show should be spent in preparation, including plaiting your horse's mane if you have an exceptionally early start on the day itself. The mane can be kept clean overnight by putting an old stocking or the leg of a pair of tights over the plaits, held in place by fixing a rubber plaiting band over each plait.

then, despite the rider urging on the horse with very positive leg aids, he gradually became more backward thinking, until he landed over one fence and almost immediately started to back off the next, which possessed a particularly unattractive and unusual filler. On the third approach the rider managed to persuade the horse to jump (albeit from a virtual standstill), but nappiness had now set in and the horse refused to approach another fence with a filler in front. The result was elimination.

The verdict Knowledgeable friends who were watching assured the rider that it was not her riding that had been at fault. The horse had been very nappy, but there was no genuine fear on his part.

Although elimination in one phase of a horse trials means elimination from the competition, it is often possible to complete the event provided you seek permission from the organizers. This was the case here.

Cross country

As a result of discussions with her experienced friends, and bearing in mind that the horse and she had had little cross country experience together, the rider decided to change tactics. Up to this point she had been very sympathetic, but she was keen to ensure that their cross country round was a positive one. As the horse had been nappy for no valid reason in the showjumping, the rider decided to wear spurs for the cross country. Her plan was to ride the horse forward much more, so that he had less chance to back off the fences and nap.

Working in The first few practice fences resulted in half-hearted efforts from the horse, so the rider touched him with her spurs, sent him on and jumped several fences out of a very strong canter. The result was a different horse to the one seen in the showjumping ring.

On the course The question was, could the rider keep this up all the way round the course? Fence one had a downhill approach, so while sending the horse forward the rider had also to keep him together, so that his hindlegs were coming well under his body and he was able to jump easily. She did not want to give him any excuse to stop. A few strides out she felt the horse hesitate, so she used her legs strongly and gave him a slap with her whip. They sailed over fence one, but a fairly tight right turn to the nearby second fence gave the horse the opportunity to fall out through his left shoulder, despite the rider's outside leg being very strong and positive. However, a speedy slap on the horse's bottom and a quick re-presentation at the fence showed him that his rider meant business.

For the rest of the course the rider had to work hard, with extremely positive leg aids, but the horse jumped everything well out of his stride – and actually started to enjoy himself!

The verdict Once the horse realized that messing about was not going to be tolerated, he settled down to his job well. The rider's ability had not increased dramatically between the showjumping and cross country phases, but her mental attitude had changed. There is a fine line between being a sympathetic rider and being ineffective: our rider became much tougher with her horse (but not cruel). All she asked was for the horse to do as he was told and to concentrate on his job for a few minutes. This is not too much to ask, when you consider that this particular rider had spent huge amounts of time, money and effort in looking after her horse.

Overall verdict and action plan

Despite the disappointment in the show-jumping, our rider learned a great deal from this first day. She determined never again to be 'conned' by the horse working well in the warm-up areas, and decided to adopt a positive, forward attitude all the time and not to relax once in the ring

SUMMARY

■ Assess yourself and your horse honestly and constructively.

■ Do not allow yourself to be bullied into pursuing goals which are not really of interest to you. Enthusiastic friends and instructors can sometimes be overbearing, so remember that you should enjoy your horse in your own way.

■ Have an action plan for your schooling sessions and even your hacks. Every ride can be used to teach your horse a valuable lesson; conversely, if you adopt a sloppy approach your horse may learn something negative every time you ride him.

Hacking can be an educational process as well as a pleasure.

simply because the horse had worked well outside.

The rider also decided to deal with any silly nappiness immediately, rather than give the horse the benefit of the doubt. If there were genuine fear of something then she would encourage him, but the first event had shown that her horse liked to pick and choose his monsters (for example, the dressage boards) and try it on with his rider.

Having made these assessments, the rider decided on the following action plan:

- Continue with lessons in all disciplines, ensuring that a positive attitude is adopted by the rider at all times.
- Take the horse out and about competitively as much as possible. This will place the rider in situations where she needs to be positive in order to ensure that her horse behaves, and by her continually adopting this attitude the horse should learn to obey the rider's requests at all times. Remember that horses learn by repetition, so repetition of bad behaviour can be detrimental – incentive enough for any rider to ensure that he or she rides as well as possible at all times. If you let your horse get away with misbehaving too often, how can you expect him to do as you say at all?

Lessons to be drawn from this real-life example

- The power of the rider's mind is tremendous, but is often overlooked. Once our rider realized that her riding was not at fault she switched into a different mental approach, forgot her worries about inexperience over the cross country and concentrated on her riding.
- Help on the ground is invaluable: had this rider not had the benefit of her knowledgeable friends' advice, she could easily have convinced herself that the horse was genuinely frightened and that it was her riding which was at fault.
- Whether or not things go as planned, you can always learn from the experience.

ACTION POINTS

- Look back through your answers to the questions at the start of this chapter and decide on your competition action plan.

- Set yourself goals and work out a strategy to reach them.

- Remember the power of your mind – check out sports psychology books for more tips on using a positive attitude to your advantage.

- Book some lessons with an experienced instructor so that you can structure a schooling programme for your horse – and yourself.

- Take the opportunity to visit clinics and demonstrations given by top riders.

THREE

Preparation – Horse Care

In addition to ensuring that your horse is supple, obedient and forward going when ridden, you will need to pay attention to other aspects of horsekeeping if you are to compete successfully.

MANAGEMENT SYSTEMS

There are several different ways of keeping horses.

At grass

In this system, the horse lives out at grass all the time, in a field which should be suitable for the purpose with secure, safe fencing, shelter from the worst of the elements, a good, clean water supply and adequate grazing.

Owners of grass-kept horses should visit their animals at least twice a day, and they should also provide extra hay and concentrates according to the horse's workload and the time of year. During late autumn and winter the nutritional content of grass is negligible and hay must be provided.

Many horses and ponies compete 'off grass' at all levels, and this includes both eventing and endurance riding. However, they will need supplementary feeding in order to provide the energy required for their work.

Stabled

Some owners are unable to turn their horses out at certain times, while some unfortunate animals are kept stabled for the majority of the year. Being confined to a loose box for 24 hours a day, every day, is not natural – horses enjoy their liberty, and the freedom to just wander along grazing. If possible, a stabled horse should spend at least some of his time at liberty; if this cannot be in a field, then turning out in a yard or school is still preferable to being stabled all the time. Any horse, whether competing or not, will benefit from time at liberty to just 'be a horse'.

Combined system

Under this system, the horse is stabled at night and turned out by day (this can be reversed in summer). Many owners operate this system, because it allows them to control the horse's weight (for instance in spring, when the grass is lush) but also gives the horse time out to enjoy himself and helps to prevent him becoming too fresh when ridden, as might be the case if he were permanently stabled. This system can be particularly satisfactory for a horse that is competing regularly.

Each owner will have his or her own preferences, and in addition may be

Work out a routine which allows you to fit in all your daily horse care tasks.

constrained by the facilities available. Working owners have the added pressure of fitting in their horse around full-time employment. On top of this, each horse is an individual and his particular needs must be the primary consideration. Do not let tradition or accepted practice become a millstone around your neck: where there's a will there's a way, so do not become bogged down in thinking that you cannot possibly go eventing because your horse has to live out!

HOLIDAYS

Just as you need a break from work, so your horse will appreciate time off, too. Each week he should have a rest day, and at some point in the year he will probably need a holiday. You will need to fit this in with your own commitments and the demands of your chosen discipline.

FEEDING AND GROOMING

Two essential components in preparing a horse for competition are feeding and grooming.

Feeding

Without the necessary supply of nutrients the horse will be unable to perform the work expected of him; he also needs a certain amount of feed each day just to maintain the status quo – keeping his bodyweight stable, the gut flora in his digestive system healthy, and all the organs of his body working efficiently.

A horse needs to eat about 2.5% of his bodyweight each day just for maintenance.

For example, a horse which weighs approximately 455kg (1,000lb) will need 11.4kg (25lb) of food every day. Before you can compile a ration you therefore need to work out how much your horse weighs. One of the simplest ways of doing this is to invest in an equine weightape (available through some saddlers and equine mail-order catalogues). Simply measure the horse's barrel by placing the tape just behind his withers and reading off the weight. You will probably find that the tape also tells you the horse's daily food requirement.

Once the overall ration is known, you can then decide what foods to include in it. There are several rules of feeding to consider:

1 Feed according to the horse's age, type and work.

Unfortunately, many people overfeed their horses, placing added strain on the animal's heart, lungs and limbs. This is not good, particularly if you then expect the horse to compete.

Horses should be well furnished but neither fat nor thin. You should be able to feel the animal's ribs easily but not be able to see them. If you have to press your fingers through a layer of fat in order to locate the ribs, then the animal is too fat. Other signs of obesity are pads of fat in the withers area, on the neck, behind the shoulder, and on the back and quarters. At the other extreme, a thin horse will have his spine, croup, hip bones and ribs prominent. There will be no muscle on him and his skin will 'stare' instead of having a healthy shine.

There are various conditions in between the two extremes, but at either end of the spectrum the horse cannot be a successful competition animal. In fact, at the worst end of the conditioning scale, the thin horse will be struggling simply to stay alive.

One of the best ways to learn about the condition expected for competition horses is to go to the top events and look at the successful horses. Event horses are leaner than dressage horses, but they carry well-developed muscle. Endurance horses are considerably leaner than many other competition horses, but they again are muscled-up and healthy. At one time there was criticism of the excess condition carried by show horses, but there now appears to be a move towards more sensible conditioning of animals for the show ring, with the horse's welfare becoming the primary consideration in this – and indeed all – equestrian sports.

Always feed according to the work done, not what you *hope* to do with the horse. Giving an animal a few extra oats the day before his competition will make absolutely no difference – the horse's feed programme needs to be adjusted as his fitness progresses, so that he always receives sufficient nutrients to meet the increased needs of his body.

Younger and older horses have different dietary requirements to those in the mid-age range. This is because youngsters are growing and need feed to meet their system's requirements for forming a strong skeletal structure, while older horses may have trouble maintaining weight or digesting certain feeds and so their diets need careful consideration in order to ensure that their higher protein needs are met.

2 Feed plenty of bulk.

The equine digestive system is designed

to cope with the horse being a grazing animal. For the majority of the day the horse is eating and his digestive system processes the food almost continually – it is estimated that horses graze for 16 hours out of 24. When your horse is stabled for long periods you therefore need to meet his requirement for bulky food in the form of forage – hay, haylages or, in times of hay shortages, hay replacements and extenders.

A horse who is out at grass for the day will be grazing, but when he comes in for the night he will have upwards of 12 hours in confinement, so you must make hay available to him during this time – if the horse's digestive system is not kept occupied with bulk food it will start to break down.

Grass is the most natural bulk food for your horse, and during spring and summer you will find that he is not overly interested in hay (although you must still give him a supply if he is stabled overnight). However, in winter the nutritional value of grass is negligible and time out at grass serves more as a period of relaxation than being of any benefit in terms of feeding.

3 Imitate nature and feed little and often. As already noted, the horse eats for a large proportion of the day, sending small amounts of food continually through his system. Once you stable him and keep him according to your convenience, you interrupt this natural pattern. If you then give the horse a huge feed just once a day you will be going against everything for which his system is designed. In compiling your horse's feeding programme, you therefore need to understand his natural way of feeding and try to replicate it. For example, you can give four small feeds rather than one big one, and provide hay for the stabled horse in the early morning, at midday, in the afternoon and in the evening, rather than in one large net. As far as possible, try to stick to a similar routine on competition days. Give the horse his largest feed and largest haynet at night, so that he has plenty of time to digest it and will be occupied during the long night hours.

Of course, working owners will have their other, non-horsey commitments to consider, but if you plan ahead it is surprising what you can arrange. For instance, my horses live in a livery yard which is close to where I work. They are out during the day and in at night all year round. Normally they are given hay and feed in the morning and at night. However, proximity to work means that during winter I can nip out at lunchtime or in the early afternoon to get them in and give them feed and hay. Other possibilities are to arrange for the yard owner or a friend or relative to feed your horse for you. You could even invest in one of the automatic feeding machines which are now available!

4 Feed only good-quality feeds.
Mouldy hay or feed will cause health problems for your horse, so don't risk a large vet's bill in order to save a few pennies on a bale of hay. Always shake out the hay before you feed it so that you can detect any mouldy bits.

Keep your hard feed in vermin-proof bins to eliminate contamination problems. Empty the bins thoroughly before putting in fresh feed, otherwise you may accumulate some fairly horrible bits of feed at the bottom. The feed manufacturers mark their bags with a 'best before' date, so check this when you are buying.

5 Ensure that your horse has a constant supply of fresh, clean water.

A horse can last for longer without food than he can without water, which is essential for so many bodily functions. Horses can be quite fussy about water – many do not like to drink out of dirty or tainted containers, so one of your daily tasks should be to clean your horse's water buckets thoroughly. This also ensures that you empty the bucket rather than just topping it up continually. Standing water absorbs ammonia, so always give your horse a fresh, clean supply.

If your stable has an automatic waterer, do check it daily to make sure that it is working. Some horses do not

like the noise made by these devices, so reassure yourself that your horse does actually use it by watching until he does. If there is any doubt, leave him with buckets of water.

Get to know how much your horse drinks so that you can leave him with enough water overnight. On average, a horse will consume 36 litres (10 gallons) in 24 hours. Soaking the hay generally causes a reduction in water consumption, but it is up to you to know your own horse, for a reduction in water intake is often a sign of ill health.

It is sensible to take your own water to competitions, particularly if your horse is fussy and may refuse to drink 'strange' water. Traditionally, horses were not allowed access to water immediately before or during strenuous work, but research in the endurance and eventing spheres has shown that water intake during competition is beneficial rather

Take supplies of food and water to the show, as you may be away from home for a long time. A horse loses a considerable amount of fluid through the stress caused by travelling, and if he becomes dehydrated he will not be so able or willing to perform.

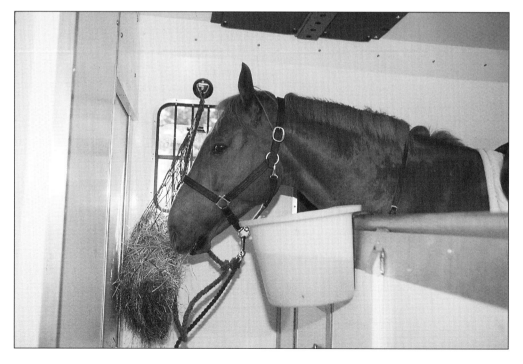

than harmful. In addition, in hot, humid conditions it is vital to rehydrate your horse throughout the competition.

6 Do not exercise immediately after feeding.

Give your horse time to eat his feed and then another hour on top before you work him. This is because once work starts, digestion stops. The horse's lungs also function better when he is not working on a full stomach – just think how you would feel if asked to do a 10-km (6-mile) run minutes after finishing a huge Sunday lunch! If the horse is going to be working really fast and hard, then a gap of three hours should be left between feeding and work. Owners who have to exercise horses before going to work can always give their horses a small handful of feed and a few carrots before they ride, and then their proper breakfast afterwards.

On competition days, arrange your feeding times to ensure that your horse is fed with plenty of time to digest his meal before he has to be ridden.

7 Feed at the same times each day.

Horses are creatures of habit and expect to be fed at their normal times. They do not know that breakfast is late because their owner has overslept: all they know is that their clock told them breakfast should have been served at 8am and no-one has yet appeared. With some horses, a feed not appearing on time is a source of real stress, which can manifest itself in 'vices' such as box walking or weaving, so do make sure you arrange sensible feeding times and stick to them.

If your weekly programme involves riding the horse first and giving him breakfast at 8am, then make sure you feed him at the same time at weekends as well. Do not (as many owners do) turn up two hours later at weekends, ride for a couple of hours and then feed the horse. By the time he gets his breakfast it will be four hours late! Instead, feed the horse at 8am as usual and get on with tasks like mucking out, filling haynets and getting in hay and straw for the week, while your horse digests his breakfast. Then around 9.15am you can ride and everyone will be happy.

On competition days, stick to your routine as far as possible, although you will have to adjust it on some occasions to fit in with your 'performance' times.

8 Always weigh your feeds.

As you will discover later (see pages 42–3), you will need to know exactly how much feed of each type your horse is getting. The only way you can do this accurately is to weigh the feed. A spring balance is handy for weighing haynets, while you can simply weigh a level scoop of hard feed. Borrow the kitchen scales or use your spring balance to weigh an empty bucket, then add a scoop of feed so that you know how much that particular type of concentrate weighs. Do not blindly follow the information given in books, because different scoops will hold different quantities of feed.

9 Introduce any new feed gradually.

If you make sudden changes in your horse's diet, the microbes in his hindgut will not be prepared and will be unable to utilize the feed correctly. This can lead to digestive upsets, some of which may be serious. You therefore need to prepare the gut flora for changes by introducing new feeds into the diet gradually. For example, a horse who has been stabled all winter should not just be thrown out into the field in spring and left there all day. His time out at grass should be limited at first, building up over several days to being turned out all the time. The same applies when bringing the horse back in, or when changing feeds: do everything gradually.

10 Consider the horse's temperament.
Altering your horse's feed cannot change your horse's basic character, but it may exaggerate it. For example, an already fizzy horse will become even livelier if fed high-energy feeds and is likely to boil over in the excitement of the show ring, whereas a cobby type is likely just to become fatter if you stuff him full of energy foods, and if he is then asked to exert himself in competition extra strain will be placed on his limbs, heart and lungs.

However, it is possible to compile a ration which provides all the necessary nutrients for the horse's workload without exaggerating any problems of temperament or constitution. There is a very wide range of feeds available, and as different animals respond differently to cereal feeds it is very much a case of trial and error, although you can reduce the risk factor somewhat by consulting an equine nutritionist. The major feed companies employ nutritionists, who run telephone helplines so that you can seek their advice. You will also find that many of these companies have stands at major events, often staffed by the nutritionists, who will be happy to advise on your specific problems. Go prepared with details of your horse's weight, current feeds, workload and so on.

11 Think about the rider's ability.
You need to be honest about yourself here – for some reason there are people who feed event cubes to their hack and then wonder why the horse is rather lively on their rides out! Overfeeding your horse and over-horsing yourself is a recipe for disaster, especially if you are aiming to compete, as a horse that becomes too lively and difficult to handle in the excitement of a competition may dent your confidence.

Formulating a ration

All the above points need to be considered in putting together your horse's daily ration. Going back to the 455kg (1000lb) horse which needs 11.4kg (25lb) of feed daily, you now need to decide how much of this should be fed in the form of forage and how much as concentrates. There are some generally accepted proportions, which are as follows:

Type of work	Hay (%)	Concentrates (%)
Maintenance/ resting	100	0
Light (hacking for one hour)	75	25
Medium (schooling/jumping)	60	40
Hard (hunting three days a fortnight/eventing at lower levels)	50	50

A horse in light work should therefore receive 75% of his ration as hay and 25% as concentrates; if he is then fittened for showjumping competitions, the hay should be reduced progressively to 60% and the concentrates increased to 40%; and so on.

Choosing concentrates

Which concentrates should you feed your horse? You may already have a preference for a particular manufacturer, and if you have bought a new horse you should find out which feed brands he has been receiving. Otherwise, read through the advertisements in magazines, contact a manufacturer and talk through your needs with the nutritionist. Does the company employ caring, practical horse people? If the nutritionist rides, then s/he should have a better understanding of the working owner's problems and needs. Is the quality of the feed good? You may know someone who uses the feed; if so, what are their views on it? How easy is it to obtain in your area?

Consider also the type of feed that you want to use. Horse feeds are now available as pellets or nuts, coarse mixes (like muesli) or extruded feed (in which the cereal is cooked under high temperature and pressure to make the feed more digestible). You may also see micronized feed: this process has the same effect as extrusion, but the cereals are cooked by ultra-red rays – similar to cooking food in a microwave.

Coarse mixes, nuts A reputable manufacturer will produce these feeds from good-quality ingredients and will balance the ration for you. This means that all the necessary vitamins and minerals are included – all you need to do is feed them! These feeds are much easier to use than 'straight' feeds and are therefore more suitable for inexperienced owners. In addition, coarse mixes and nuts are easier to store than straight feeds, requiring fewer vermin-free bins in order to create the overall ration.

Extruded and micronized feeds These have the same advantages as coarse mixes and nuts, but they are also more easily digested.

Straight feeds (oats, barley, etc) With these feeds, the onus is on you to ensure that your horse's ration is balanced, and this may be difficult as each bag of feed will be slightly different. You will therefore have to make some assumptions about the feed, and will need to look up the facts about digestible energy, protein content and so on in a detailed feeding reference book. All this makes it much more difficult to ensure that your horse's ration is balanced properly. On the other hand, feeding must be tailored to the individual horse, and some may refuse to eat nuts at all, so you will need to make your final selection according to your horse's preference and needs.

With all this information at your fingertips, you can now make an informed choice. Then talk to the relevant company's nutritionist again to check that your feeding plan makes sense.

Using supplements

An extraordinary amount of money is spent each year by horse owners on feed supplements, but how much of this is really necessary? If your horse is receiving a quality feed from a reputable manufacturer and is eating the recommended amounts, then he ought to be receiving all the necessary minerals and vitamins. However, if you are feeding

HAY AND HAYLAGE

CHOOSING HAY

The nutritional value of your hay will depend upon several factors, including where it was grown, at what stage it was cut, and how it was dried and stored. Although there are certain pointers to note to help you distinguish between good and bad hay, the only accurate way to discover its nutritional value is to get it analysed scientifically. Feed companies will be able to advise on this.

Good hay is greeny fawn in colour, contains good grasses (such as timothy, ryegrass and meadow fescue), smells pleasant and shakes out easily, is free from dust and mould, and springs apart when you open a bale.

Bad hay contains weeds and poor grasses, smells musty, may be damp or mouldy, and is very stalky. Yellow or dark brown hay which smells sweet is mowburnt – that is, baled before the grass has dried properly.

Avoid hay which has been taken from poor land, as the grasses will be poor. Ragwort may also be present, and this is even more poisonous in its dried state than when growing.

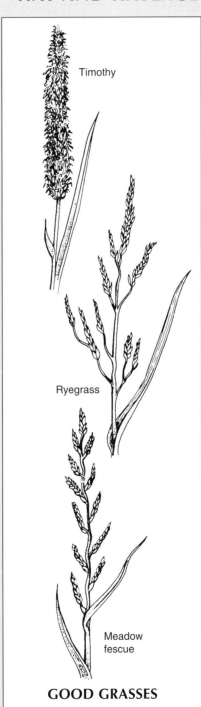

Timothy

Ryegrass

Meadow fescue

GOOD GRASSES

STACKING HAY

Buying hay in bulk straight off the field is the cheapest way of obtaining your hay supplies. When you stack it, take care to leave spaces between the bales so that the air can circulate and assist in the drying process. This also reduces the fire risk. Stack hay on wooden pallets, again leaving spaces in between. Do not stack hay on plastic sheets, as this could result in overheating and a fire.

HAYLAGE

Take note of the manufacturer's warning on the bag that haylages should be used within five days of the bag being opened. If a bag has been damaged, perhaps by piercing with a stable tool, and then left to stand, the contents should not be fed but should be disposed of safely.

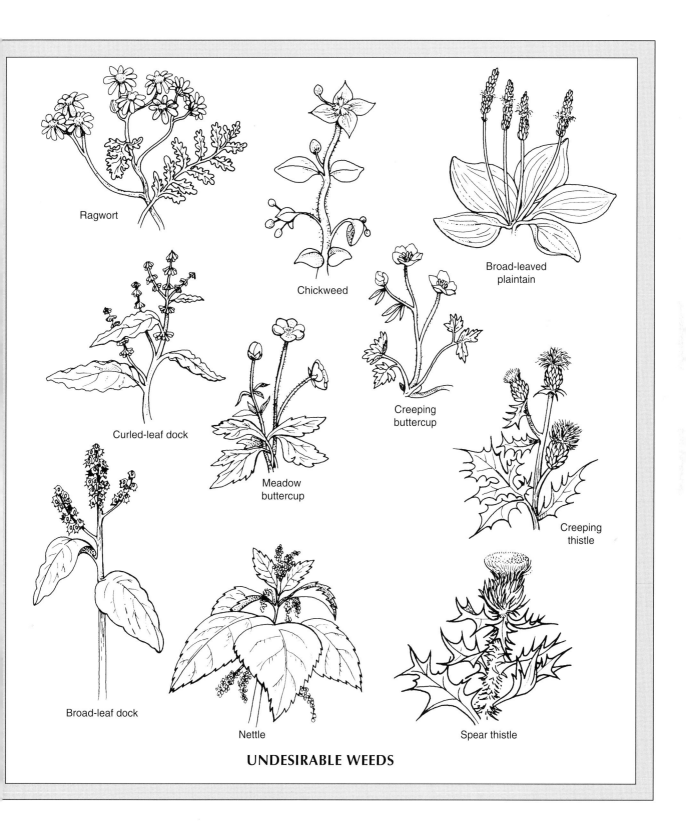

Ragwort

Chickweed

Broad-leaved plaintain

Curled-leaf dock

Meadow buttercup

Creeping buttercup

Creeping thistle

Broad-leaf dock

Nettle

Spear thistle

UNDESIRABLE WEEDS

FEEDING TIPS

- Use a weightape to check your horse's weight on a weekly basis. You will then know if he is losing or gaining weight. It is virtually impossible to do this accurately by eye alone.

- Adjust your horse's feed if his needs change.

- If the horse is off work, cut down his hard feed. There are also a number of convalescent diets available which ensure that your horse gets all the required vitamins and minerals during his recuperation.

- Remember that a sensible worming programme is vital to complement your horse's feeding regime.

- Have your horse's teeth checked at least once and preferably twice a year. If he cannot chew his feed properly it will not be utilized fully and you will be wasting money. More importantly, your horse could be suffering

'straight' feeds, such as oats or barley, or are feeding a prepared feed at lower levels than those recommended by the manufacturer, your horse would benefit from a general vitamin and mineral supplement.

Salt is something that is added by most owners – a tablespoon per day mixed into the feed is sufficient. Garlic is another popular extra; it is reputedly a mild anthelmintic (wormer), acts as a deterrent to flies and helps with respiratory problems.

If your horse has specific problems, such as with the quality of his hoof horn, then your vet, farrier or nutritionist may recommend a supplement that will help to deal with this.

Worming

Every horse has worms, but if the burden gets out of control serious problems may ensue. As a responsible owner you should worm your horse regularly: every eight weeks in winter and every four to six weeks in summer. Horses pick up worms from pasture and even from stable floors, so your worming programme has to be a rolling effort to keep the parasites under control.

At specific times of year certain action is necessary. In midsummer and mid-autumn, a double dose of a wormer containing pyrantel is needed to control tapeworms; in late autumn to early winter you should use ivermectin against bots; and in the latter part of the year a five-day course of a fenbendazole wormer is recommended to battle against encysted redworm. Throughout the rest of the year, ordinary doses of wormer are used. You will need to know your horse's bodyweight in order to work out the correct dosage.

Wormers come in granule or paste form. The former is mixed into the feed, the latter is administered by inserting the nozzle of the syringe into the side of the horse's mouth, so that when the plunger is depressed the paste is deposited on the back of the horse's tongue. The taste of wormer in feed can be disguised by adding sugar beet.

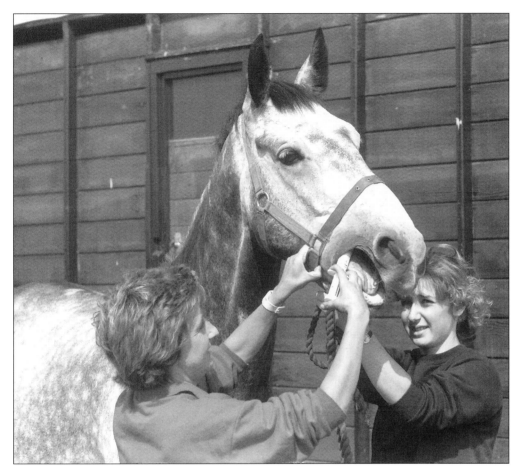

Worming can be carried out via a syringe, whereby the paste is deposited at the back of the horse's mouth, or using granules mixed into a feed.

Grooming

Grooming is an essential part of your horse's daily care and is carried out to keep his skin in good condition, improve muscle tone, maintain his general appearance and improve his circulation. The skin is, in effect, the largest organ of the horse's body, providing a protective covering for tissue. It helps to eliminate waste products from the horse's body, and for a working horse – whose systems are subject to stresses not imposed on resting or wild horses – regular grooming assists in this process. If the horse lives out all year grooming will be minimal, as you do not want to remove too many of the natural oils which protect the horse against the elements. Stabled horses and those who spend part of the day outside can undergo more thorough grooming programmes.

Grooming regimes

All horses should be groomed daily. However, the extent of the grooming will depend on their lifestyle.

At grass

- Remove mud and dirt from the horse's coat before riding.
- Pick out the feet at least once a day.
- Sponge the eyes, nose, sheath or udder and dock daily.

Daily attention to your horse's feet is essential.

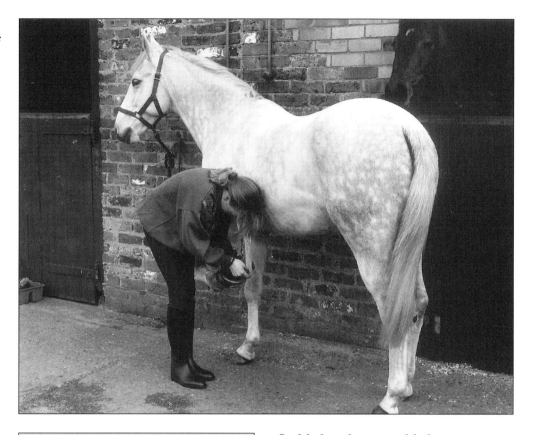

GROOMING TIPS

Do not brush your horse's head while he is tied up. Undo the lead rope, but leave it looped through a breakable piece of string, then undo the headcollar and buckle it around the horse's neck while you brush his head.

■ Always use the hoof pick from heel to toe.

■ Remember to clean a gelding's sheath or a mare's udder regularly. Baby wipes are handy for this purpose.

Stabled and part-stabled

- Remove dirt and sweat marks before riding.
- After riding, remove sweat marks caused by the saddle. Sweat is acidic and can cause a reaction in the horse's skin, leaving it susceptible to rubs and friction.
- Pick out the feet twice a day.
- Sponge the eyes, nose, sheath or udder and dock daily.
- Groom thoroughly (30–45 minutes) every day if possible, although working owners may find this difficult.

If you are competing in showing classes you will have to spend more time grooming, and will need to make use of some of the specialist products available, such as show sheens.

GROOMING KIT

Your grooming kit should include the following items:

Sponges   Use separate ones to clean the horse's eyes, nostrils, sheath or udder and dock. They must be kept clean. Alternatively, use separate pieces of cotton wool and dispose of them immediately afterwards.

Dandy brush   This brush is used to remove mud and dirt. As the bristles are coarser and do not remove as much grease from the coat as those of the body brush, it is ideal for use on grass-kept horses. Do not use it on the mane or tail, however, as the hairs will become split or broken. An old dandy brush is ideal for brushing away bits of loose dirt and bedding once the horse's feet have been picked out.

Rubber curry comb   This is useful for removing unwanted hair when the horse is changing his coat and for loosening dirt.

Body brush   This brush does most of the work of grooming, as the short bristles get right into the coat and remove dirt and scurf. It is used in conjunction with a metal curry comb, the comb being used to clean the brush following every four or five strokes.

Water brush   This is useful for removing stable stains on light-coloured horses and for laying the mane flat.

Hoof oil and brush   These are used to enhance the appearance of the horse's hooves.

Mane and tail comb   These are used for pulling the mane and for dividing it up for plaiting.

Sweat scraper   This is used when the horse has been washed down after exercise or bathed, to remove the excess water.

Shampoo and tail oil   There is a wide variety of shampoos on the market, plus 'anti-tangle' oils which are helpful in separating a knotted tail. Baby oil is also good for this.

Stable rubber   An old linen teacloth is perfectly adequate and is used to wipe over the horse after grooming.

FARRIERY

All horses require the services of a farrier, but if you are competing regularly it is even more important that you have a good relationship with your farrier. In some sports, particularly endurance riding, the horse will wear out his shoes very quickly, but as a general rule his feet will need to be attended to every four to six weeks.

The above applies whether or not your horse is in work, and whether or not he has shoes on. The horse's feet are growing constantly and will need regular trimming by a good farrier to ensure that the hoof remains balanced. If the foot is allowed to get too long, this in turn places extra stresses on the tendons and ligaments. The old saying of 'no foot, no horse' is very apt.

There are a few common courtesies you can pay your farrier to keep him happy and aware of you as a caring, considerate customer:

- Provide a well-lit place, preferably with concrete standing, where your farrier can work.
- Have your horse ready and waiting for him: it is amazing how many people expect the farrier to trudge across a field and catch the horse before he shoes it.
- Have the horse's feet picked out and ensure that his legs are clean – presenting a horse with wet, muddy legs is not conducive to good relations.
- Be there to look after your horse, including holding him if he is particularly difficult about having his feet done.
- Pay the farrier on time and give him plenty of notice for the next visit – he does have other clients to look after.
- If you have a youngster, it is your duty to handle the horse and get him used to having his feet picked up. It is not the farrier's job to educate your horse.

When your horse is on his annual holiday and is turned out to grass, you may be able to remove his shoes completely, but do consider the condition of his feet and of the ground before rushing to do this. Some horses are always best left with at least their front shoes on, as otherwise they may become footsore.

DENTISTRY

Even in countries where there are no formal qualifications for equine dentistry, such as the UK, there are people who attend to horses' teeth. Some of these, by virtue of experience and their own efforts to learn, do a good job; others do not. (Currently there are two master dentists in the UK who are qualified by virtue of taking examinations in the USA, where there are recognized qualifications for equine dentistry.) Find your equine dentist by word-of-mouth recommendation and then satisfy yourself that he is doing a reasonable job by carrying out a simple check.

When your dentist attends to your horse he will need to feel the horse's teeth in order to know what work is required. Ask if you too can feel the teeth (the horse's premolars and molars), and then repeat the procedure once the work has been done. If the horse's teeth still have sharp edges on them, the work has not been completed properly. In addition, if your dentist does not use a gag on the horse then he cannot possibly get right to the molars at the back of the jaw.

Vets can also attend to your horse's teeth, although their charges tend to be higher.

SADDLERY

Being basically genuine creatures, horses tend to put up with all kinds of discomfort. Some of them even perform to a reasonable level despite the fact that their tack is uncomfortable, or the rider is insensitive, or the horse is in pain for some other reason. In order to compete successfully you have to learn to pay attention to detail, and that means everything from how your horse is feeling to whether you are using the right bit for the relevant competition.

PERMITTED BRIDLES

As rules may change from year to year, it is wise to check the rule book for your discipline annually.

Dressage

Bridles

- Preliminary and Novice – ordinary snaffle

- Elementary to Advanced Medium – ordinary snaffle or double bridle

- Advanced – double bridle

Nosebands (drop, flash or cavesson) must be used with a snaffle bridle. Grakle nosebands are permitted only in horse trials dressage tests.

Bits

- Ordinary snaffle with jointed or double-jointed mouthpiece

- Eggbutt snaffle with or without cheeks

- Rubber snaffle

- Unjointed snaffle

- Snaffle with upper cheeks

- Hanging cheek snaffle

All parts of the bit coming into the horse's mouth must be made of the same type of metal. Bit guards are not permitted.

Other tack

Breastplates are permitted, but boots, bandages and martingales are not.

Horse Trials

- Rules for the dressage phase are as for pure dressage (above), although grakle nosebands are permitted.

- For the jumping sections, running or Irish martingales are permitted. Gags or hackamores may be used, as may tongue guards.

Showjumping

- Standing and running martingales are permitted. The former must be attached to a cavesson noseband.

- There is no restriction on bits, but the rules state that 'no item of saddlery or equipment is to be misused'.

Endurance

- A recognized form of bridle must be used, with or without a bit.

As far as saddlery is concerned, it is important that your tack fits the horse well, is suitable for you and the particular discipline, and is in good condition. Poorly fitting saddles can cause considerable pain for the horse, although some horses have a high pain threshold and simply carry on, coping as best as they can.

To check whether your saddle is affecting your horse, work him on the lunge without any tack. Watch carefully how he moves:

- Is he tracking up?
- Is he coming through from behind with one hindleg more than the other?
- Does he have a good length of stride?
- Is he swinging through his back?

Once you have acquainted yourself with that picture, add the saddle and see if there are any changes:

- Does the horse now shuffle along?
- Have you stopped him coming through so well from behind?

If there are very obvious differences, it is highly likely that the saddle fit is not as good as it should be.

Now examine the saddle fit further. Stand the horse on level ground and fit the saddle without a numnah, but with a girth.

- Does the saddle have clearance all along the horse's spine? At least three fingers' width between the withers and the pommel should be allowed, and this clearance must still be there when the rider is on board.
- Look at how the saddle fits around the horse's shoulder: does it sit so far forward that it interferes with the movement?
- Does the saddle press into the horse? You ought to be able to run your fingers down from the pommel, in between the saddle and the horse, without too much difficulty. If you feel your fingers are being squeezed, how will the horse feel, especially when a rider is on top?
- Stand back and look at the saddle. Is it too long for the horse and pressing on his loins?

- Is the saddle level? Look at the pommel and cantle: if one appears lower or higher then the saddle is not sitting level on the horse.
- Look at the back of the saddle: are the panels sitting flat, so that the rider's weight will be distributed over a large area, or will all the weight be concentrated on a couple of places which will soon become pressure points?

Now take hold of the saddle and see how stable it is. If it moves around too much, then it is highly likely that it does not fit particularly well.

It is now time to ride in the saddle – this gives you a chance to discover whether the saddle fits *you*. If you have encountered problems earlier and have called in a professional saddle fitter to check out your saddle, at this point s/he will be able to see how the horse moves in the saddle. If a horse that has been used to a saddle which pinches because it is too narrow is then fitted with a saddle suitable for it, the difference in movement is unbelievable; it is like having a new horse, especially as once he realizes that he can move freely he will do so, showing off extended trots and standing off from fences where before he may have just crept into them. You will need to ride for 15–20 minutes and then check the fitting again. A good saddler should be able to bring a selection of saddles for you to try and ought to offer an after-sales service as well. As the horse changes shape owing to muscle development and gains or loses weight, which may be particularly marked if you are competing in, say, endurance riding, so your saddle may need to be adjusted.

As a general rule, you should have your saddle checked at least once a year in case any reflocking is necessary. This is also a good opportunity for someone with an experienced eye to check for damage: it is not unknown for a broken tree to be missed by a less knowledgeable rider. If you and your horse have fallen, it is also sensible to get the saddle checked for damage.

SPECIALIST SADDLES

You can compete successfully using an ordinary general-purpose saddle, but most riders who are really serious will want to buy a suitable saddle for their chosen discipline.

TACK CLEANING

Naturally, cleaning tack is part of your preparations for a competition, but everyday care is also required. Always wash off the bit after it has been used, and if you can get into the habit of wiping over your tack each time as well this is extremely helpful. Such a habit makes the weekly strip-down of tack to give it a really thorough clean much quicker.

When you take your tack apart, check everything for safety: stitching, billets, where leather is bent over and where the girth straps are attached to the saddle tree. If something needs repairing, get it done immediately; otherwise, you could find yourself involved in a totally unnecessary accident.

Use a damp sponge to wipe off dirt and grease. For bits which are difficult to

SYNTHETIC TACK

Synthetic tack has come a long way since it was first introduced. New leather-look styles are now available and in a variety of types. If you have a hectic life, synthetic tack – which is virtually maintenance free – can be extremely useful. It is also less expensive than leather.

remove, a ball of rolled-up tail hair is effective and does not damage the leather. To apply saddle soap, use a dry sponge and wet the soap rather than the sponge. This prevents you from creating too much of a lather, which simply wets the leather rather than treating it. Ensure that the underside of the leather is well

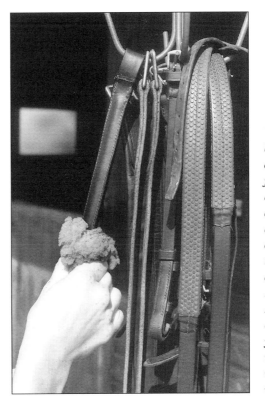

There is more to being a successful competitor than just the riding, and attention to detail in all aspects of horse care – including tack cleaning – is essential. If you look after your horse and carry out all the tasks yourself, you will ultimately achieve more satisfaction when you succeed.

ACTION POINTS

- Allow time in your daily programme to groom your horse thoroughly.

- Keep a planner on your tackroom wall to ensure that you stay up to date with farriery appointments, worming and vaccinations.

- Get to know the rules on tack for your particular sport, remembering to note the changes from year to year.

- If your horse is competing regularly it is worth having his back checked throughout the year. There are some very reliable back specialists around – word-of-mouth recommendation is best when it comes to choosing a specialist.

treated, as this is more absorbent. If your tack has got wet, allow it to dry naturally – do *not* place it near artificial heat. It may then be necessary to oil the leather; in any case, you should oil your tack a couple of times a year.

If you make sure that you maintain this standard of tack cleaning, you should not need to do anything extra for competitions other than polish up buckles and stirrup irons. Using metal polish on bits is not a good idea.

TACK-CLEANING TIPS

- If your tack needs to be stored, apply a dressing to keep mould at bay.

- Use a sterilizing fluid to disinfect secondhand tack before you use it and to get rid of any mould before a saddle is cleaned properly.

SUMMARY

- Feeding, grooming and basic health care all play their part in the preparation of a competition horse.

- Attention to detail is vital in all horse care, irrespective of whether or not you are competing.

- There is plenty of expert advice available on feeding and saddle fitting, so take advantage of it.

FOUR

Fit for Work

If you had never run in a race before but had decided to take part in a marathon, you would not just turn up on the day and hope for the best. Months of preparation would have seen you gradually improve your running skills and the distances covered, so that you were as well prepared as possible for the race itself. Yet many riders adopt something of an 'unprepared but keep your fingers crossed' approach when it comes to their own and their horse's fitness for competition.

INCREASE YOUR KNOWLEDGE

You can never know too much about fitness. Take advantage of the information provided in books such as this one, talk to more knowledgeable competitors and, most importantly of all, 'listen' to your horse. The only way to learn about fittening is by doing it, but you must have a plan of action in order to give you some guidelines to follow. Always be prepared to adjust your programme according to what your horse is telling you via his condition, vital signs, health and behaviour.

You may feel that as you are only taking part in the local hunter trial you do not need a properly structured fitness schedule, but preparation is still vital if your horse is to be able to give of his best and enjoy the event. It is also simpler to keep track of what you have and have not done if you write it down. An understanding of the basic principles of building fitness is also a prerequisite for every horse owner.

FIRM FOUNDATIONS

Your horse's fitness needs a solid foundation, which means lots of slow work in the early stages. Boring though it may be, walking exercise is vital as the first step to fitness.

If your horse has had a long lay-off, he will need plenty of slow work in order to accustom his body to working again; his return to fitness will be a gradual process, and if you try to rush the early stages you may cause more damage and find yourself back at square one. The importance of this cannot be overstated: I know of an event horse who was off work for twelve months following a tendon injury and, after consultation with the vet, it was decided that he could be brought back into work. Although the horse

WALKING *CAN* BE INTERESTING

You can make your horse's walking exercise more interesting for both of you if you select your routes carefully. Take in some of the more attractive villages in your area, box your horse to more interesting scenery, or incorporate some simple school work, such as leg yielding and transitions, into your hacks.

would never be able to event again, the vet felt confident that he would be able to cope with general riding club work. Unfortunately for the horse, the owner decided to put him out on loan, with the specific proviso that he was to be used for light hacking only. The rider who took him knew the horse's history and promised that she would bring him back into work gradually, which to any sensible person would mean at least a month's walking exercise, gradually building up the time and keeping a careful eye on the horse's legs. However, within three weeks the rider had taken the horse hunting: not surprisingly, his tendon again broke down and this time the prognosis was not good. The horse was effectively ruined.

The example above demonstrates that the important point to remember about building fitness is to tailor the work to suit the particular horse's needs. If your horse has been off work for a long time due to injury, it is obvious that his muscle tone will have deteriorated, his heart and lungs will not have been exerted and he will generally be in soft condition. Do check with your vet and take his advice.

Even if your horse has only been off work for a short time he will still need to start with walking exercise, but you may be able to move up the fitness ladder a little more quickly. At all times, it is the horse who will be able to tell you whether you are progressing too quickly or not fast enough – but you have to know how to read the signs.

BEFORE YOU START

Before embarking on any fitness programme with your horse, you should carry out the following:

- Check your horse's teeth. They may need rasping so that he can gain the maximum benefit from his food – remember that fittening not only involves the work that you give the horse, but is also closely related to his feed and general management.
- Ensure that your horse's vaccinations are up to date: you will need a valid certificate to get on to some showgrounds and to register your horse with various competitive organizations. As the horse can only be worked lightly for a few days after vaccination, it makes sense to get this done before he even starts work.
- Get your horse shod.
- Monitor the horse's pulse, temperature and respiration rates (see pages 57–59). You will need these in order to know how his fitness is progressing. You should take the readings at the same time each day for a week in order to obtain a good average.
- Take note of your horse's vital signs: TPR (Temperature, Pulse and Respiration), eye and nostril membrane

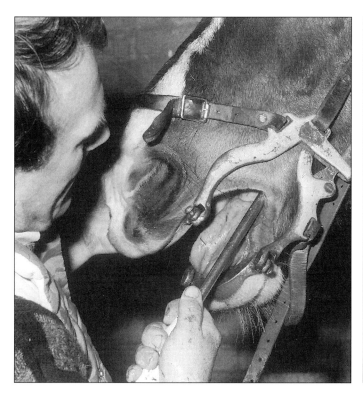

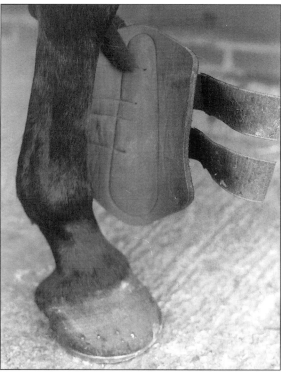

colour, state of his droppings and urine, coat condition and general manner, to ensure that there is no doubt about his health.

- Make sure that you know your horse's legs. Feel them so that you are aware of every lump and old wound; then, if anything does start to go wrong you will know right away. As a matter of course, each time you finish riding check your horse's legs, looking for signs of heat, any cuts and so on.

- Weigh your horse: using a weightape is the simplest and cheapest method (see page 38). Although not as accurate as a weighbridge, provided you use the same tape all the time you will have a good idea of any weight gain or loss.

- Assess your horse. Stand back and take a critical look at him. What kind of condition is he in? Does he have a huge grass belly after a summer out at pasture? Alternatively, is he rather lean? As your horse works, he will need food in order to supply the necessary energy, and his condition prior to starting work will have an effect upon the amount of food he should receive (see Chapter 3).

- Worm your horse regularly as a matter of course (see page 46).

- Ensure that your saddle still fits your horse properly (see pages 51–52).

- On a horse in soft condition, use a synthetic padded girth rather than a leather one.

- Put protective brushing boots on your horse as a precautionary measure.

Pulse

Your horse's pulse can be taken in the following places:

LEFT *Before you start your horse's fitness programme he needs a general health check, correct shoeing, worming and a visit from an equine dentist.*

RIGHT *Brushing boots are a sensible protective measure to employ every day.*

Familiarize yourself with your horse's pulse rate at rest, so that you can monitor it and use it as a guide to his developing fitness.

- Where the median artery crosses the jaw.
- Just behind the elbow on the inside of the leg.
- In the girth area on the left side.
- Under the dock.

It is easier to locate the pulse in the first

three, although you will need a stethoscope to hear it in the girth area. In the first two you can feel it with your fingers – do not use your thumb, as your own pulse will confuse matters! Count the beats for 15 seconds and then multiply this by four to give you the beats-per-minute total. If you do use a stethoscope you will hear the heart making a 'lub-dubb' sound, which is equivalent to one beat.

The normal range for a horse at rest is 36–42 beats per minute, but each horse is an individual and this is why it is important to know what is normal for your horse. The pulse of a foal will be higher, while the pulse of a very fit horse will be lower than that of a horse in average work.

Temperature

Temperature also varies from horse to horse and will be slightly higher in the afternoon than in the morning. The climate will also affect a horse's temperature, as will exercise, which will raise it. To ensure that you have an accurate record, you should therefore take your horse's temperature at the same time each day and as far as possible under the same conditions – you cannot control the weather, but you can remember to do a temperature check when the horse is at rest rather than after work. The norm is 38°C (96.8°F), although individuals will vary slightly. Any rise or fall in a horse's normal temperature requires further investigation in case a health problem is brewing.

Respiration

Your horse's respiration rate can be measured by standing three-quarters on

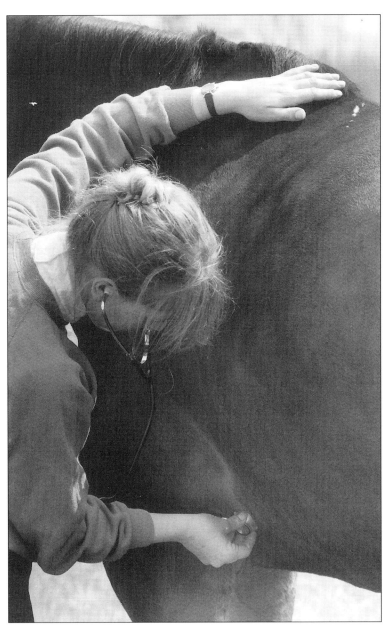

to his flanks and watching them rise and fall. Each rise and fall counts as one respiration: again, the weather conditions can have an effect, so bear this in mind. Measure the horse's respiration rate at rest so that you have a base figure for comparison. The norm is 8–12 breaths per minute.

Later on you will be able to assess your horse's fitness by using these three sets of figures, so it is vital that you know what is normal for your horse before you start the fitness programme.

EARLY WORK

Weeks 1–2

You should start your horse's fitness programme with walking exercise, preferably on smooth roads to avoid the possibility of tweaking a tendon or causing a sprain, which can happen on a soft or uneven surface, and you should build up over a week from 30 minutes to one hour. The horse must be encouraged to walk out properly rather than just slopping along. Do not try to put him 'on the bit', but you should have a contact and ensure that he walks forward from your leg.

Increase the walking exercise over the next week so that by the end of two weeks your horse is walking for 1½ hours, and is coming back feeling lively. If you have access to long, slow inclines this is useful, as walking uphill will make the horse use his muscles, heart and lungs to greater effect. Make sure that when going up and down hill you keep the horse balanced.

Roadwork can be extremely dangerous – the roads are not the place to be if your horse is nervous or flighty.

Weeks 3–4

Short periods of trotting can now be introduced. However, if your horse is returning to work after a long lay-off you must continue with the walking exercise, taking longer to build up the time.

When trotting, ensure that you use decent surfaces: trotting along rutted bridleways will result in a sprain or strain. Try to avoid working on excessively hard ground, as concussion is a factor in some foot problems. However, if you are hunting or competing in endurance riding your horse will need to trot on the roads, so it makes sense to incorporate this into your preparation. Time your trotting periods and build them up each day. When trotting, take note of the horse's breathing as part of your regular monitoring of his fitness programme.

Be vigilant about checking your horse's legs throughout his fitness work, but particularly after each new step up the fitness ladder. After each week of the programme, check the horse's pulse, temperature and respiration, and check his weight.

In the third or fourth week, some schooling work can be introduced. Some riders use schooling in preference to roadwork or hacking for fitness purposes: for example, former Olympic event champion Matt Ryan very rarely hacks out on his horses, preferring to improve their suppleness through work in the school. Later on, he uses gridwork and canter sessions. His methods certainly work, as anyone who has seen his horses competing will know. There are many options and you should keep an open mind, learning and adapting ideas to suit your horse's individual needs.

Under the 'standard' fitting pro-gramme known and used by many riders, the fourth week may also see the introduction of canter work.

Weeks 5–10

Over the next four weeks or so, more canter and jumping sessions can be introduced gradually, along with dressage schooling periods.

Following this programme, if you are aiming at eventing for example, at the end of 8–10 weeks the horse will be fit enough to cope with a fairly demanding cross country course, a dressage test and a showjumping round all on the same day.

INTERVAL TRAINING

Interval training was developed originally for human athletes, but has been adapted for horses and is proving extremely successful. This technique takes the guesswork out of getting a horse fit as it consists of set work periods, executed at a specific pace and speed, interspersed with set rest periods. In the rest periods the horse is allowed to recover partially before being asked to work again, so that his tolerance for work is gradually increased without the levels of stress becoming too high.

Interval training requires monitoring of the horse's pulse and respiration rates to provide a guide to the amount of stress he is under. The work periods are short, so the risk of injury and 'anaerobic' respiration is reduced. Anaerobic respiration occurs when the horse's energy demands are greater than can be supplied by the oxygen arriving in the blood. In this situation, the muscle tissue has to use glycogen reserves to produce energy

Don't forget to have fun, otherwise getting your horse fit for competition can take over all your time with your horse, to the detriment of your enjoyment of each other.

without the aid of oxygen. This is not only inefficient but also results in the production of a toxic waste product called lactic acid. This contributes to fatigue and therefore limits a horse's athletic performance. The aim of getting a horse fit is to enable him to work 'aerobically' (when the oxygen supply in the blood is adequate to supply the energy demands), so that he can carry on for longer before anaerobic respiration and lactic acid build-up result in fatigue. Interval training develops the horse's aerobic capacity, and as the work periods are short there is less chance of injury and fatigue.

Before starting interval training a horse will need the basic foundation of fitness work – that is, four weeks of walking and trotting.

RIDER FITNESS

While riding in itself will have an effect on your fitness, it is also helpful to incorporate sports such as swimming and circuit training, especially if you are aiming to take part in competitions such as endurance riding or eventing.

The other important point to remember is to warm up before you mount. As mentioned earlier (see page 28), we give our horses a loosening and stretching period before starting serious work, and should do the same for ourselves.

SPECIMEN FITNESS PROGRAMMES

The following examples of fitness programmes give guidelines only and should be adapted for each horse and rider's individual circumstances. As already emphasized, time spent on the foundations of fitness work is vital – do *not* be tempted to take short cuts. You should also bear in mind that young horses will take longer to get fit than seasoned campaigners; again, do not rush the early work or impose too many strains on a youngster. Ideally, you want your horse to enjoy many competitive seasons and rushing him early on may shorten his working life. All the programmes assume one day off work each week.

TIME AND MONEY

You may need to invest time and money in getting your horse fit for certain disciplines. For example, if endurance is your interest, you may have to travel to other areas in order to work your horse on hills or to be able to put together long, interesting rides. Eventers may have to hire gallops, perhaps from a local training centre, if they do not have access to suitable going for their faster work.

Showjumping
Weeks 1–2 Roadwork, building up from 30 minutes' walking to one hour in the first week, and to two hours by the end of the second week.

Weeks 3–4 Continue with walking on the roads, but introduce some schooling sessions in the arena or field. These can last for around 20 minutes and involve walking and trotting. Before starting a schooling session your horse should be warmed up, so you could hack out first and then school him. The amount of schooling your horse needs depends on his age and his level of training, an experienced competitor needing less than a youngster who is still being educated.

Some people are happy to introduce trotting periods into their roadwork, while others are against this owing to the increased concussion on the horse's limbs.

Weeks 5–6 Canter work and more intensive schooling sessions can be introduced during this phase, along with some jumping. Gridwork can be used to increase the horse's agility and confidence, as well as building the correct musculature. Do not overdo the jumping, however: a couple of sessions is enough for the fifth week, with three or four in the sixth.

Canter work should be increased gradually over these two weeks. The showjumper will have to execute tight turns at speed in competition, so it is important that his flatwork and jump schooling include exercises to help improve his suppleness and obedience.

Some horses may be ready for a small competition by the end of their sixth week.

Weeks 7–8 Assuming that your horse is competing on one day per week, vary his work programme with hacks out, schooling sessions and no more than a couple of jumping sessions per week.

Dressage
Weeks 1–4 As for showjumping.

Week 5 onwards Periods of schooling can be lengthened or varied with lungeing. Ideally, sessions should total around 40 minutes per day; however, if you hit problems you may need to work through the difficulty, the aim always being to finish on a good note. Be careful not to spend too much time working the horse in the arena so that he becomes sour, and give him regular breaks to allow his muscles to relax after the exertion. Intersperse your schooling with hacks out, gridwork or loose-jumping sessions – there is no reason why your horse should not jump even if his major discipline is dressage. As a general guideline, aim for eight weeks of work before taking the horse to his first show.

The dressage horse needs suppleness and power, and building the correct muscles and muscle tone to compete at a high level will take years of systematic training.

Eventing
Weeks 1–2 As for show-jumping.

Weeks 3–4 Start to introduce short trots into your two-hour hacks. For example, trot for just under two minutes on the first day of week 3, then incorporate

Lungeing is a useful exercise if you are short of time to ride. Always work on a good surface.

Side reins are attached once the horse has been warmed up on both reins. These provide a contact for him to work into.

When you have finished lungeing, undo the side reins and attach them to the dee-rings on the saddle.

two two-minute trots on the second day, and so on. At the same time, gradually reduce the length of the hacks, so that by the end of week 3 the total time is $1\frac{1}{4}$ hours and includes two five-minute trots.

Week 4 will consist of four days of hacks lasting $1\frac{1}{4}$–$1\frac{1}{2}$ hours, including three five-minute trots. The other two days will incorporate an hour's hacking at walk, plus a schooling session of 20 minutes.

Weeks 5–6   You can now introduce canter and pole work. Time will still be spent hacking out (including walk, trot and short canters), as well as longer schooling sessions of 30–40 minutes. In week 6 small jumps can be used as part of the schooling. Gradually build up the canter work, so that by the end of the week your horse can happily cope with a $1\frac{1}{2}$-hour hack including two three-minute canters. These canters should be strong, forward-going work – do not allow the horse to slop along.

Your horse should now be fit enough to cope with a dressage or small showjumping competition.

Week 7   If you use interval training, this can now be introduced and used once every four days. The horse should still be hacked out and schooled on the flat and over fences.

Weeks 8–12   The programme continues with a mixture of one-hour hacks plus schooling and twice-weekly jumping sessions, including some cross country work. Interval training will progressively build up the time spent in canter.

Your aim is to complete your first horse trials at the end of the twelfth week.

Whether you pursue the interval-training route or not, before your horse goes to his first event he should have completed at least four sessions of faster work in the build-up to the competition.

Endurance

Most horses who are reasonably fit can complete a 24km (15 mile) pleasure ride without too much trouble, but for the longer, faster rides more serious preparation is required. If the horse has not been properly prepared he may suffer serious distress; it is also important that the rider is fit, as a tired rider is a heavy burden for a horse to carry.

As endurance horses need to go on at a steady pace for many miles, it is important that their initial conditioning work (the first stages of any fittening programme) is longer than advocated for other disciplines. It is also beneficial to work over varied terrain, in order to prevent boredom for both horse and rider and to help the horse's muscle development, for example by working up hills.

Up to 48km (30 miles)   If your horse is currently hacking fit, you will need another couple of weeks in order to prepare for a 32km (20 mile) pleasure ride. Should that go well, and you set your sights on a 48km (30 mile) ride (average speed 9.5kmph/6mph), you will need a further two to three weeks of preparation. You will have to build in longer training rides of up to two hours, with several miles of trotting at a good pace (around 13kmph/8mph) and more canter work. Include these longer rides on at least two days of your week, with the shorter rides incorporating short, sharp canters. At this level, do not let the

Working your horse up and down inclines helps him develop balance and muscle.

average speed of your rides exceed 16–19kmph (10–12mph) or you will stress your horse.

Up to 64km (40 miles) The next step is to 64km (40 mile) rides and again extra time will be needed. Remember that your horse is an individual and must be treated as such, with your fitness programme being adjusted to cater for his particular needs. Four weeks would probably be needed to progress from 48km (30 mile) to 64km (40 mile) rides, using a six-days-per-week exercise programme involving longer rides at faster speeds. For example, two weeks before the 64km (40 mile) ride the horse should be able to do a 40km (25 mile), 32km (20 mile) and 32km (20 mile) ride on consecutive days, at an average speed of 11kmph (7mph). In the week prior to the competition it is important not to overdo the training – ease back on the speed and simply keep the horse ticking over, with the most strenuous ride being 32km (20 miles) in the middle of the final week.

Longer rides Preparing your horse for the longer rides, up to 160km (100 miles), can take several months.

Setting the pace
When preparing your horse for endurance, it is important to know how fast he can travel, comfortably, within the various paces. A walk averaging 6.5–8kmph (4–5mph), with the horse relaxed and free striding, is important, as the walk is used as the 'rest' period in endurance riding. At trot and canter the horse will have a certain speed at which he is happy, and it is not advisable to push him out of his comfort zone as going faster than he finds comfortable will be tiring for him. A slow trot will be

KNOW YOUR HORSE

It is vital that endurance riders really know their horses and make use of pulse and respiration readings to gauge fitness levels. These readings should return to normal within 30 minutes of finishing work.

TROTTING TIP

When covering long distances, it is vital that you remember to change the diagonal frequently when trotting.

ACTION POINTS

■ Monitor your horse's TPR and weight, and use these observations as guides to his health and fitness.

■ Note down your horse's progress in a diary – you cannot remember everything that happens over a long season.

■ Visit competitions as a spectator and look at the condition of the top horses to help you develop an eye for what is required in your sport.

around 9.5–11kmph (6–7mph), a strong trot will average 14.5–16kmph (9–10mph). If your horse's trot is not his best pace and he is rather slow, you will have to make up time by using canter: a rolling canter will average about 16–19kmph (10–12mph).

It is important to note that the above programmes are guidelines only and that each horse's fitness schedule should be worked out according to his individual needs. In learning how to fitten horses there is no substitute for practical experience. However, if your experience is based upon sound principles, the horse can only benefit.

SUMMARY

■ Prepare your horse before you even start a fitness programme.

■ Always ensure that the foundations of your fitness programme are sound. The initial slow work will provide a firm base upon which to build, whichever is your chosen discipline.

■ Speed – especially if introduced too early in the programme – can result in tendon breakdown and respiratory problems.

■ Monitor your horse's progress carefully throughout and listen to him: there will be signs if you are taking things too quickly, such as slow recovery after workouts, heat in the legs, stumbling when working or reluctance to continue. Keep a written record.

■ Work on your fitness too!

FIVE

Travelling

All the preparation in the world is useless if your horse refuses to be transported to your chosen competition. It is most unnatural for a horse to enter a confined space which is above ground and moves at considerable speed, making turns and strange manoeuvres, bumping over rough terrain, grinding to a halt every now and then, and swaying as other vehicles scream past – yet we expect the horse to put up with all this without making a fuss, and come out at the other end ready to perform well in competition.

Simply walking into a trailer or lorry is a huge act of faith on the horse's part, for in doing so he is overriding all his natural instincts. Horses are naturally timid animals who prefer to run away rather than fight. In the wild they have large areas in which to live, so they can escape from danger. If they come across something strange, they approach it warily, look at it, sniff it and eventually touch it repeatedly, in order to establish whether or not it is dangerous. At the same time, their innate sense of self-preservation tells them always to have an escape route, so that if danger looms they can get away with their lives.

These basic instincts are still very strong in the horse, but all too often we fail to acknowledge or take account of them. However, when handling any horse, and especially when trying to load him into a trailer or lorry, it is important that you understand life from the animal's point of view.

There is really no point in forcing a horse into a trailer or lorry. It may work for a few times, but gradually the horse's resistance will become stronger and stronger, and in a battle of strength the horse will always win. If your horse is genuinely frightened of the trailer or lorry (and remember that a fairly dark, low place can make him feel claustrophobic), then hitting him will only confirm and reinforce his initial fears of the vehicle.

You must use your superior brain power to set up a situation in which the horse learns that loading into the vehicle is not something to be feared. This will involve a great deal of time and patience. You cannot effect a quick cure, so if your horse is a poor loader you will need to work on this problem well before you intend to get out and about.

TEACHING YOUR HORSE TO LOAD

When setting up your vehicle for teaching your horse to load, take note of the following:

Practise loading at home so that you know your horse will walk into the box happily on show days.

- If possible, position the trailer or lorry alongside a wall or fence so that the horse can only duck out one way.
- Make the vehicle as appealing as possible: remove the partition, and open the front unload (if there is one) or the groom's door.
- Ensure that the ramp is on level ground, so that it does not move and feel unsafe when the horse puts his foot on it.
- You may need to spread straw or other material from your horse's bed on the ramp, as some animals do not like this strange black expanse in front of them.

Set aside all day and have a helper who will be as patient as you. Use a bridle or controller halter for extra control if your horse is a bargy type, and have some feed in a bucket to act as a bribe. Now walk your horse up to the ramp. If he is genuinely afraid and refuses to go anywhere near the vehicle, you may need to park it in his field for a few days (or weeks) and make a point of letting him graze near it. Then lead him around it until he becomes so used to it that it is no longer a monster.

If the horse will walk up to the ramp and then digs in his heels, play the waiting game. Do not let him graze or go backwards, but do let him sniff and touch the ramp if he wants to. Use the feed to encourage him forwards, praising him each time he takes a step in the right direction. You may not get very far on the first day but do keep trying – three times a day or more if necessary – as long as you can stay patient. Take the view that the horse is going to get bored before you do! With some scared horses it can take days before they make it up the

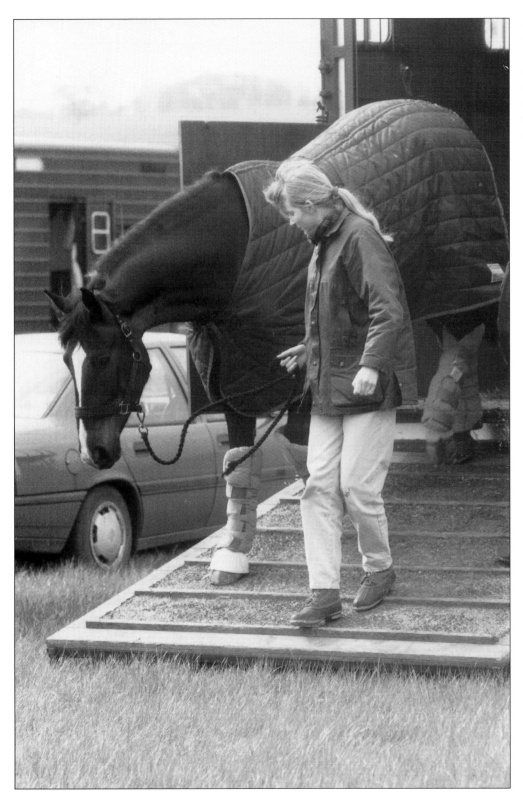

Be careful when unloading – walk the horse down the ramp, taking care that he does not go off at an angle and jolt himself unnecessarily.

ramp, but if you force them to go you are only confirming their worries. They have to make the decision themselves.

Eventually you will be able to get the horse into the lorry or trailer: one of my horses took a week before he would go in and out happily. When introducing a colt who was only a few months old to travelling, I saw the horse's natural behaviour at first hand – he sniffed the ramp, tasted it and then pawed it vigorously before trusting it enough to place a foot on it. The colt was allowed to sniff and taste the ramp as he slowly made his way up, doing everything at his own speed. Once in, he was allowed to lick and chew the interior: some people would tell him off for this, but it was simply his way of finding out whether or not everything was okay and of letting the lorry (and us) know that he was okay with everything. He did not actually damage anything, because his chewing lasted for only a few seconds and he moved quickly from the lorry sides to the partition, the window and so on. Had we not allowed him to satisfy his curiosity in this way, but told him off for chewing, he would have associated the lorry with punishment and we would have created a problem for ourselves. As it was, the whole process took 30 minutes at the most, and this included taking the colt on and off the lorry several times so that he was loading like an old hand.

Once you have the horse in, do not be too keen to take him off on a trip. If he is claustrophobic, you may find that he goes in and immediately backs out again – and determining whether a horse is genuinely frightened of being closed in or is just being difficult is not easy. When faced with such a decision, consider the horse's other behaviour to identify whether or not there are any signs that he suffers from claustrophobia.

Build up gradually so that you can load the horse happily, put up the ramp, reward him and let him stand for a while (talking to him for comfort if needed) before unloading again. When all this can be achieved without fuss, you can take the horse for a short journey.

If all goes well, longer trips can then be undertaken, perhaps unloading and reloading at a friend's yard or other different but safe location, before you go to a show. Always allow plenty of time at the show, because with all the excitement and distractions loading may take a little longer.

OTHER LOADING METHODS

A good introduction to loading and travelling at an early age sets the tone for the horse's future, and there is no doubt that a horse who is good to load and well behaved in the lorry or trailer is a real asset.

However, not all horses have this opportunity, and some which know better may still persist in being tricky to load. If your horse is just being awkward, then lunge lines attached to the sides of the vehicle and crossed behind the horse's quarters by two helpers usually work. If you are alone, it is also possible to attach a line to one side of the trailer and lay the rest out in a loop around the ramp, so that you can walk the horse towards the ramp, pick up the end of the lunge line with your free hand and bring it up so that it is around the horse's quarters. You have to be adept to exert pressure with the lunge line and hold on to the horse, but with a reasonably well-behaved horse this method works well.

A rope device, consisting of a piece which goes over the horse's back just behind the withers and loops on to a continuous rope that passes either side of the horse and around its quarters, flanks and shoulder, finishing in two loops, works just as well. The handler holds on to the horse's headcollar with one hand and has the two loops in the other. She can then keep the horse straight and exert pressure on his quarters to move him forward.

HIRING TRANSPORT

Hiring may be a more economic proposition than having your own transport if you do not plan on doing a great deal of travelling far afield. Check out your local saddlers and newspapers for details of haulage firms in your area. Some national magazines also take advertments for horse transport services.

LORRY OR TRAILER?

While financial constraints will obviously have a bearing on your choice of transport, each has its own advantages and disadvantages.

Lorry
For:
- A lorry is a more stable method of transport for the horse, generally giving him a more comfortable ride.
- It is much easier for the driver to manoeuvre.

- Often the driver can see or hear the horses in the back, which is useful if anything is amiss.
- Many lorries have living areas as well, so you will be more comfortable at shows, and if you have to stay away you have your accommodation on hand.
- As a lorry is larger inside, it is easier to tack up the horse while still on board if necessary.
- Storage space inside the lorry means that you do not have to fill your car with horsey gear.
- A lorry can be multi-purpose. For instance, it can be used for carting hay or bedding, or even for moving house!

Against:
- The initial cost of a lorry is often higher than that of a trailer, although some smaller lorries can be picked up fairly cheaply.
- You will still need your car.
- Lorries need to be plated every year.
- You will have additional road tax and insurance to pay on a lorry .
- If you do not have room at home, you may have a problem finding some-where to keep a lorry. Not all livery yards have facilities, and if you have to make alternative arrangements this may involve an extra cost, although some establishments charge whether you have a trailer or a lorry.
- A lorry will need servicing regularly.

Trailer
For:
- The initial investment is lower than for a lorry.
- It may be easier/cheaper to find a space to park a trailer.

- No road tax or insurance is needed.
- Maintenance costs are usually lower than for a lorry.

Against:
- A trailer is less stable than a lorry, and therefore less comfortable for the horse.
- The vehicle is detached from the driver, so you may not know if the horse is in trouble.
- If you have two horses in a trailer, your equipment will need to be carried in the car.
- It is not so easy to prepare a horse for competing in the confines of a trailer.
- Most horses load more easily into a lorry than a trailer.
- You need to learn the knack of reversing!

Whatever you decide to buy, do check the ramp and the flooring of the container. Replacing a rotten one will involve a considerable investment.

The towing vehicle

If you have opted for a trailer, the first thing to do is to ensure that your car can cope with the towing. If it can't, you will be putting the car passengers, the horse and other road users at risk.

You can find out the trailer's weight by checking the handbook and the chassis plate. Add on the weight of your horse – the total must not exceed the trailer's maximum gross (laden) weight. You will also need to know how much downward pressure the trailer puts on the tow hitch (known as the trailer's laden noseweight) – you will find this in the trailer handbook, or you can consult the manufacturer.

Once you have all this information, consult your car handbook to work out whether or not your car would be a suitable towing vehicle. You need to know the car's maximum towing weight, its kerb (unladen) weight and the maximum trailer laden noseweight.

A sensible option is for the car's maximum towing weight to be 85% of its unladen weight. If you exceed this there is more chance of an accident, as the trailer may well start to dictate what happens to both itself and the car!

It is dangerous to assume that a four-wheel drive vehicle will automatically tow a trailer – I know that my own would not stand a chance of towing a pony in a trailer, never mind my horses. This is because the engine is not powerful enough, the car is too light, and if someone did attempt to tow with it the trailer would soon be dictating the fate of both vehicle and trailer.

If you are going out to buy a car specifically for towing a trailer, make sure you do your homework so that the salesman's patter does not override safety considerations.

Driving a lorry or trailer

Even if you will not be driving your vehicle yourself, it is useful to bear the following points in mind and make sure your driver is aware of them.

- If you have never towed before, you will need to practise with an empty trailer before you take your horse out in it.
- When towing a trailer or driving a lorry, make sure that you look and think ahead so that you can slow down and brake earlier for roundabouts,

turnings, bends and so on. Apart from allowing time for emergencies and for a trailer making it more difficult to slow the car, it is worth remembering that the horse does not know when a roundabout or bend is coming up, and consideration on your part will make his journey more comfortable.

- Take corners smoothly and carefully in order to give the horse a chance to keep his balance. Always allow extra room for your trailer, so that you avoid hitting the kerb.

- When negotiating gateways, again remember to allow for the extra width of your trailer.

- Use your mirrors – then you won't be taken by surprise if a truck or coach zooms past. Resist the temptation to overcorrect if caught in the slipstream of a large vehicle.

- Remember that many other motorists have no idea about towing trailers or driving lorries and may put you in difficult situations. Think and look well ahead to avoid disaster.

- Do not drive for more than two hours without stopping. Check that the horse is okay and offer him water. Always stop and investigate if you hear strange noises coming from the lorry or trailer.

- Do not drive across a field as if you are on a nice smooth road – *slow down*.

- Make sure you know how high and wide your lorry or trailer is. Then you will know whether or not you can fit under that bridge!

- Keep your trailer secure when not in use by using a wheelclamp and/or other security measures, such as your postcode in huge letters (which cannot be removed) on the roof.

- Make sure you carry a spare wheel and that it is legal.

- Observe the legal speed limits for vehicles towing trailers.

- Make sure that the car and trailer tyre pressures are correct before you move off.

TRAILER 'SNAKING'

This is a horrible experience whereby the trailer starts moving about from side to side. If you do nothing, there is the chance that the trailer and car will go out of control. Equally, resist the temptation to do anything drastic (like braking hard). Instead, ease off the acclerator and make small corrections with the steering wheel until you regain control. If this happens on several occasions, get your trailer checked over.

TRAILER TECHNIQUES

Hitching up a trailer

- Before you start, make sure that the trailer hitch will clear the car's towball. Remove any covers on the trailer and car and unclamp the trailer if it is secured.

- Reversing your car so that the towball lines up with the trailer hitch can be a fairly tricky operation. If you have a helper with you when you are hitching up, ask her to stand alongside the trailer and indicate to you where the hitch is by holding up her arm – you will then know where you are aiming. Reverse slowly so that you can adjust your line if necessary.

- Your helper can indicate how far you have to go to meet the trailer hitch. Aim to get as close as possible in order to save your strength.
- When the hitch is over the car towball, lower the trailer hitch with the jockey wheel, using a bit of brute strength to make sure the two line up. On some trailers you need to hold up the locking lever, while others click down automatically to lock on the towball. You can usually hear it, but you can also check by raising the jockey wheel again to see if the back of the car lifts.
- Release the trailer handbrake before you attach the breakaway cable to the car. If you buy a secondhand trailer, make sure that it does have this cable: it is a legal requirement, as the cable is intended to pull on the handbrake if the trailer breaks free. Attach the cable to something solid on the car (not the bumper).
- Ensure you wind up the jockey wheel and that it is secure.
- Now plug in the electrics.
- Check that none of the cables will drag on the ground.
- Check that the trailer and car lights and indicators work.

If everything is fine, you can think about loading your horse.

Reversing a trailer

Many people regard this task with some trepidation, but it is a skill which can be learned quite easily following some simple guidelines. The main point is to make sure that you practise manoeuvring your towing vehicle and trailer in a large area (such as your field) without the horse on board. Allow yourself plenty of time so that you can really get to grips with reversing, and make sure your have mastered the technique well before you need to do it in public or with a horse on board.

In your field, or wherever you are practising, use a couple of cones or something similar – which will not damage the trailer or be irreplaceable if you knock into them – to mark out an area into which you will reverse the trailer.

To most people, the strangest aspect of reversing trailers is the fact that you have to turn the steering wheel the opposite way to the direction you want to go. Try to have someone guiding you back at first, and when reversing in public places always get someone to see you back, as there is a blind spot behind the trailer and it would be easy to cause an accident to people or horses.

When you start to practise, position your trailer and towing vehicle so that they are as straight as possible. It is easiest to start by reversing towards the driver's side, because if you go the other way you have to judge what is happening primarily by using the opposite door mirror. Begin to reverse slowly, turning the steering wheel *gradually* in the opposite direction to the way you wish to turn. Watch what you are doing out of the driver's window. Take everything slowly at first, so that you can learn how little steering to add in order to get the trailer to turn. It is much simpler to add a little more steering than to try to correct a car and trailer which have already gone out of line due to over-enthusiastic steering. When the trailer starts to turn, it is time to turn the steering wheel back a little – it is too late if you wait until the lining up the trailer and car with the gap marked out by the cones, so all you have to do is reverse straight back into your space. Then pull forward again and keep practising reversing through the cones until it becomes a natural manœuvre for you.

Practise reversing to the more difficult (passenger) side as soon as you have the knack of reversing to the driver's side. When you are travelling with your horse, it is far easier to reverse without him in the trailer, but if you cannot avoid this do take into account that the extra weight will make the trailer respond more slowly.

trailer is at the angle you want. Finally, you will need to steer in order to bring the nose of the car around.

You should now have succeeded in

TRAVELLING KIT

You should accustom your horse to his travelling gear before you actually take him anywhere. Some horses do object to wearing boots or bandages and you do

A cob who has been well equipped for travelling. The only addition could be a poll guard fitted to his headcollar. A leather headcollar is safer for travelling.

not want to discover this on the morning of a show or mid-transit.

Ideally, your horse should wear:

- Leather headcollar – a nylon one will not break and the horse could get hung up.
- Poll guard – available from saddlers, or you could make your own.
- Travelling boots or bandages applied over padding, all round. There is a wide range of boots available which are very quick to put on and take off. Some have knee and hock padding incorporated into them. On longer journeys, however, bandages will provide more support, but they must be applied properly.
- Hock and knee boots – if these are not incorporated into the travelling boots.
- Tail bandage and/or tail guard.

As extra protection for your horse's tail while travelling, fit a leather tail guard over the usual tail bandage.

- Roller to which the tail guard can be fastened.
- Rugs as appropriate to the time of year.
- If your horse fidgets a lot, it is also sensible to fit overreach boots all round to give extra protection to the coronary bands.

Make sure that there is sufficient bedding on the lorry or trailer floor. Some floors are not intended to have bedding added, which is fine if you know that your horse will still stale in the vehicle – some do not like their legs being splashed.

In addition to your tack, grooming kit and equipment needed for the competition itself, other items you will need to take with you include:

- Haynets and hay to last the outward and return journeys, as well as the time spent at the show if you expect to be out all day.
- Feed as required.
- Bucket and plenty of water.
- First aid kit – human and equine.
- Spare rugs.
- Any loading equipment you need.
- Skip and rubber gloves to muck out the lorry or trailer during the day (do

PRE-JOURNEY CHECKS

- Check the water, oil and fuel levels of the towing vehicle or lorry.

- Check all tyres, including the spares.

- Check the lorry or trailer flooring.

not leave your horse's droppings and bedding on the showground).

- Membership card and number if you belong to a vehicle recovery organization.
- Mobile phone or money and telephone card.
- Fire extinguisher – and know how and when to use it.

COPING IN AN EMERGENCY

Travelling your horse around in a lorry or trailer inevitably means that at some point you will have to deal with a problem or possible emergency.

What you do depends on the individual circumstances. If, for example, a trailer has overturned with a horse inside, you may place yourself in danger if you try to extricate an animal who is panicking and flailing about. If you do succeed in getting him out and he is reasonably unhurt, what hope do you have of holding on to him? You would create more problems for yourself and other road users if your horse escaped and bolted down a road.

However, there are some general points to consider in an emergency:

- As soon as the incident has occurred, use your mobile phone to summon the relevant emergency services.
- Ensure that you always carry a knife, so that you can cut a lead rope to release a horse if necessary.
- Keep a length of rope on board, as it may be needed to help extricate a trapped horse.

- Use your fire extinguishers if necessary. Incidentally, do not be too enthusiastic about a lorry with an electric ramp: one unfortunate owner lost his horses when the electrics in his lorry ramp caused a fire. There was no way of getting the ramp down to release the horses and the fire spread, with tragic results.

ACTION POINTS

- Practise driving your car and trailer or lorry without the horses on board, so that you are happy reversing, negotiating tight turns, narrow gateways and so on.

- Accustom your horse to his travelling gear before he first wears it on a journey.

SUMMARY

- Invest time in teaching your horse to load at home – kindness and patience will set him up for a lifetime of co-operation.

- Ensure that your horse is well protected when travelling.

- Keep your vehicle in good condition, paying special attention to the flooring.

- Always drive carefully so that your horse has a pleasant journey.

SIX

Show Style

There is now a huge range of showing classes suitable for all types of horses and ponies and at all levels from small village shows through riding club championships, to large agricultural shows and ultimately national titles at the major events of the season.

Many people aspire to reach the higher echelons of showing and search constantly for the top-class horse that may take them there. However, there is a great deal of pleasure and satisfaction to be gained from showing at the lower levels as well, and the bonus is that with the variety of classes available there really is something for everyone. For example, showing includes such classes as tack and turnout, working hunter pony, first ridden, cob and riding horse, and fun classes such as the pony the judge would most like to take home. Arabs, coloured horses, riding ponies, hunters, hacks, mountain and moorland – all breeds and types are catered for. Some societies have their own shows, while many of the larger shows include classes for specific types or breeds.

SHOW CLASSES

Hunters

The ridden or 'show' hunter classes are usually divided into light, middle and heavyweight, referring to the weight that the horse is capable of carrying – this is linked to the amount of bone the horse possesses (measured around the cannon bone just below the knee – a heavyweight hunter would have at least 23cm (9in) of bone and be able to carry 90kg (14 stone). In working, ladies' and novice hunter classes, the weight specifications are not so important.

Ideally, a show hunter should be the perfect horse for the hunting field: a good-looking, quality animal who is able to gallop well and has impeccable manners. In all the hunter classes the horses are galloped, shown stripped and ridden by the judge, although the riders do not have to perform individual shows. The horses must have their manes plaited, but while tails are often plaited at the lower levels, in top-level hunter classes pulling is the order of the day.

Generally, tack for hunter classes should be plain and strong. Double bridles or pelhams are suitable for the weight classes, while working hunters may be shown in either of these bridles or a snaffle, and a martingale is permitted. However, you may not change tack between the jumping and showing sections of a working hunter class.

For in-hand hunter youngstock classes,

leather headcollars or bridles are acceptable. Yearlings may be shown in mild bits, two- and three-year-olds should be bitted. Brood mares must be plaited and wear double bridles, while their foals may be plaited and should be shown in a leather foal slip.

Cobs

In recent years cobs have become extremely popular. They are usually extremely versatile, relatively inexpensive to keep and provide a great many riders with hours of enjoyment. For showing, a cob must not exceed 15.1hh and may be a lightweight or a heavyweight. Chunky, compact animals, cobs should have bone and substance. They are judged along the same lines as hunters, so must be able to gallop well and have good manners. Your

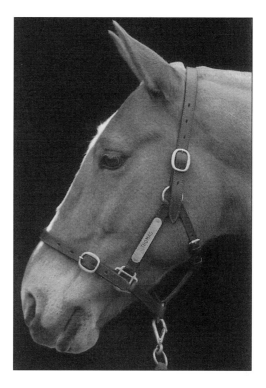

The trimmed head of a cob who is a successful all-rounder.

The same cob showing that he can jump as well as look good!

cob will need to be well schooled – if you aim for him to be a suitable mount for an elderly gentleman you will be on the right track. The judge will ride your cob.

Cobs are shown with hogged manes and either pulled or plaited tails. Double bridles or pelhams are used for straight showing classes, although working cobs may have any bridle and may also use a martingale. The leatherwork should be plain and reasonably wide.

Riding horses

In these classes the judge is looking for a quality animal with good conformation, good straight action, substance and presence. Individual shows are given, and as the judge also rides it is important that your horse is well schooled and obedient – the emphasis is on the horse's training and manners, and the ride it gives. Double bridles or pelhams are worn, with the width of leather to suit the horse, and the mane should be plaited, with the tail plaited or pulled, as for a hunter.

Hacks

The horses in these classes should give pleasure to their riders and also to the spectators – they are the epitome of grace, elegance and manners. There are two categories: small, up to 15hh, and large, over 15hh but not exceeding 15.3hh. Most horses in hack classes have a large proportion of Thoroughbred blood in them, although there are also Arab and pony types.

While hacks are not expected to gallop, they are expected to have exemplary action at walk, trot and canter. Individual shows are given but the judge does not ride. Double bridles or pelhams are worn, as for riding horses, with perhaps a coloured browband to suit the horse's coat colour. Manes should be plaited and tails pulled.

Ponies

There are a large number of classes suitable for all kinds of ponies including show ponies, show hunter ponies, leading rein, first ridden and working hunter ponies. The classes are divided according to the pony's height, with novice and open sections, so children of all ages are catered for. Check the current requirements for tack and turnout with the relevant society, as there appear to be frequent changes in fashion and acceptability.

Mountain and moorland ponies

Britain has nine native pony breeds – Highland, Dales, Fell, Connemara, New Forest, Shetland, Welsh (Sections A, B, C and D), Exmoor and Dartmoor – and there is plenty of scope for showing them in pure- and part-bred classes, ridden or in-hand. In addition to their breed classes, these ponies may also enter working hunter pony and other show classes. Some shows also provide mountain and moorland driving classes. There is no age limit for these classes, so they provide the adult pony owner with a great chance to enjoy competing on their pony.

Mountain and moorland ponies are shown in their natural state, with manes and tails unplaited. As for show ponies, check the tack requirements with the relevant society to keep your turnout up to date.

Arabians

Arabian horses have a huge following and there are plenty of showing classes for pure, Anglo- and part-bred Arabians. Once again, check the current tack and turnout requirements with the breed society.

HAVE A GO!

As there is such a variety of classes, you can always find something to try in the showing world. For example, if you possess a cob you could do straight cob showing classes, but if your horse also has jumping ability then working cob classes could be his forte. While straight showing classes put considerable emphasis on the horse's conformation, there are other factors to be considered in many classes. For instance, in working hunter classes the horses first have to jump a course of rustic fences. They must jump fluently, out of a good hunting pace, and be able to negotiate combinations and narrow fences such as stiles. Those who jump clear go forward to the next stage of judging, when their movement, conformation, manners and the ride they give the judge are considered.

In order to give the judge a good ride, your horse has to be well schooled, obedient and supple, so if your first interest is dressage there is no harm in trying something different just to keep your horse interested in his work. For instance, a riding horse class could be suitable, although at smaller shows you may have to pop over a small fence as well in this class. I know of one event horse that enjoys success in working hunter and riding horse classes at local level, while another event horse carries its rider to success in side-saddle classes!

If you have a horse of a specific breed

SHOWING A YOUNGSTER

If you have a young horse, in-hand and, later, ridden show classes are a good introduction for him. The larger shows include in-hand youngstock classes for many of the breeds and types, often further divided by age, while at the smaller events you may find just one mixed class for one-, two- and three-year-olds.

---

or type, contact the relevant society to find out if there are any shows in your area. You can then visit these and really do your homework on what is involved in showing your particular horse. This is the best way to learn about any type of showing: look at the horses' tack and turnout, the riders' or handlers' clothes and how they present the horse to the judge, how the riders use the ring and what the grooms' responsibilties are. Have a really close look at the horses placed in the top three and try to work out why they were more successful than the rest. Was it because of a horse's extravagant movement? Or because the rider executed a really flash individual show? Or because horse and rider were a workmanlike team?

The reasons why particular partnerships win will vary from show to show. If you have a horse that has reasonable conformation and moves well, then you have the chance to enjoy your showing and hopefully pick up a few prizes here and there. However, how you present your horse – in terms of both grooming and schooling – is vitally important.

PREPARATION

Horse care and grooming

To compete in showing classes your horse obviously needs to be fit, well and in good condition. His feeding and fitness programme will also include grooming (see Chapter 3), but you will need to take extra care to produce a horse whose coat really does shine. This requires effort from you in terms of strapping the horse, and you can also take advantage of some of the many show products now available to give added gloss to your horse's coat and reduce mane and tail tangles.

Trimming and plaiting

Unless your horse can be shown 'natural', untrimmed and with free-flowing mane and tail, you will need to decide how your horse should be trimmed and whether his tail should be pulled or plaited.

Ears

To trim your horse's ears, gently squeeze the edges of the ears together and trim off any protruding hair using round-ended scissors. Do not trim off the hair inside the ears, as this acts as a filter for foreign objects and is needed by the horse.

Whiskers

There is a great deal of controversy over the question of trimming a horse's whiskers. Some people do this without a second thought, while others refuse to trim off the whiskers because they are a vital aid to the horse in sensing where he is in relation to other objects, particularly at night. It is up to each owner to decide whether to subscribe to the humane or cosmetic school of thought.

Pulling a mane

A horse's mane is pulled in order to thin out and shorten it so that it is easier to plait. Many people think that a pulled mane can also look smarter and improve the appearance of the horse's head and neck. You should aim for a finished length of about 10cm (4in).

It is not a good idea to pull a mane immediately after it has been washed, as the hair is generally too slippery. Try to organize mane-pulling sessions to follow after exercise or when the weather is hot, as the hairs will come out more easily, causing less discomfort to the horse.

Brush the mane thoroughly and make sure there are no knots or tangles. Using your mane comb, and working with a small section of hair at a time, backcomb the hair up to its roots, wind a section of hair around the comb and then pull it out with a short, sharp tug. Some horses do object to having their manes pulled, so try to do a small amount every day rather than launching a major attack in one go. If your horse is really upset by the process, use a thinning comb instead to shorten and thin out his mane. Alternatively, hold the strands of hair upright from the mane crest and pull upwards. This seems to work well with horses who object to their manes being pulled.

Pulling a tail

A horse's tail is pulled in order to improve its appearance and to show off the

> ## TRIMMING TIP
>
> Trim off any hair around the fetlock and coronary band to improve the appearance of your horse's lower leg.

TAIL TIPS

- Ideally, the horse's tail should finish about 10cm (4in) below the point of hock. When assessing how much to cut off, do bear in mind how the horse carries his tail when moving.

- A pulled tail should be bandaged regularly to keep it looking at its best.

- Keep on top of the pulling by doing a little, often

hindquarters. You will notice that horses in top-level show classes invariably have pulled tails. If you decide to pull your horse's tail you will no longer be able to plait it as the hairs will not be long enough, and it will take several months for the tail to grow back to normal.

To pull a tail you need to remove the long hairs from the sides of the dock, generally pulling to about two-thirds of the way down. Before you start, ensure that the tail is well brushed and free of tangles. You should strart at the top and work downwards, taking a couple of strands of hair, winding them around your finger and then pulling sharply downwards.

As with the mane, it is sensible to pull the tail over a period of time. This ensures that the dock will not become too sore – remember that the horse will not accept tail pulling readily if he has bad memories of the last time.

Plaiting

You should practise plaiting your horse's mane and tail well in advance of your first show. Experiment with the size, number and placing of the mane plaits to discover what suits your horse and shows off his neck and shoulder to best advantage.

Bathing your horse

Horses are bathed in order to remove dirt and grease, perhaps before attending a show or going hunting, or to freshen them up after strenuous exercise in the summer – it is as quick to bathe your horse properly as it is to just wash the sweaty parts.

Most people who bathe their horses in preparation for a show do so the day before, but do remember that if you wash your horse's mane and tail they will be rather slippery afterwards and therefore not as easy to plait.

If your horse lives out you should not bathe him too frequently, as you will be removing essential oils from his coat with each wash. The weather will also play a part in your bathing routine. For example, if your horse has been hunting in winter the quickest way to get rid of the mud on his legs, belly and quarters is by washing it off. It is fine to do this provided you take him out of the wind and cold outside and dry him off thoroughly afterwards.

Select a warm day. Make sure that everything you need is to hand:

- Hose and running water, or buckets of water if your horse objects to a hose.
- Sponges, shampoo, sweat scraper, towels and appropriate rugs for drying off.
- Clean headcollar – the muck from a dirty headcollar could run into the horse's coat.
- Helper (if you are not sure how your horse will react to being bathed).

PLAITING TIPS

- When plaiting, use a wooden clip-type clothes peg to hold back the mane which is not needed when you are plaiting.

- To ensure that your plaits are even in size, put an elastic band around the comb to mark out how big each section of hair should be.

- For showing classes your plaits must be sewn in.

- If your horse has a short, thick neck, make the plaits small and tight.

- If your horse has a long, weak neck, make the plaits larger, looser and more upright.

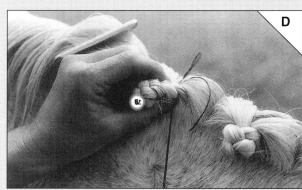

A *When plaiting a mane, start by dividing the mane into manageable sections and then dampen one of these. Split the section into three, ready to plait.*

B *Plait, maintaining the tension in order to produce a neat finished result. Your horse's mane will need to be pulled prior to plaiting so that you do not have uneven strands of hair to plait. Do not wash the mane on the day you plait, or you will find it difficult to grip the hair and maintain the tension.*

C *Sew the end of the plait.*

D *Double the plait under or roll it, according to the effect you are trying to achieve. Secure the plait with thread. Black thread has been used here so that it will show up on the photographs, but normally you would use a thread which is the same colour as the mane.*

Two plaits: the one on the left has been secured with a rubber band, the one on the right has been sewn in. For show classes you must sew in the plaits.

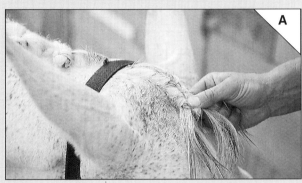

A *Plait the forelock as you would the tail in order to achieve a neat look.*

B *Double the forelock plait and then secure.*

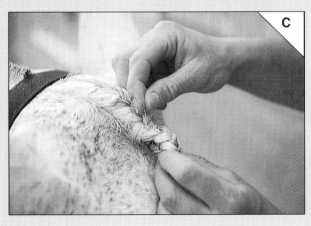

C *A neat forelock plait.*

PLAITING TIPS

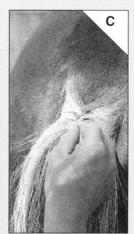

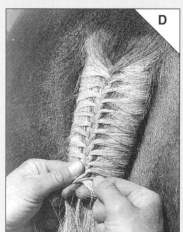
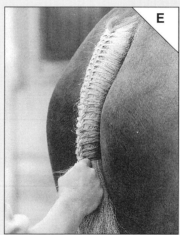

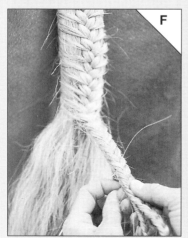
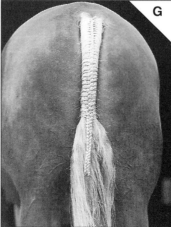

A *For a tail to be plaited it needs to be full, with the hair at the top long and preferably never having been pulled. Ensure that the tail is clean and brush and comb it well before you start.*

B *Take a section of hair from either side. Cross right over left and then bring in a third section of hair from the left. As you continue plaiting down the tail you will produce a flat central plait.*

C *Alternatively, a raised central plait can be produced. Take sections of hair from either side and a section in the middle of the tail. Take the central section over the right-hand section and the left-hand section under.*

D *As you plait down the tail, take in sections from either side.*

E *Tail plaits are meant to show off the horse's hindquarters, and you should continue plaiting as far as necessary in order to achieve this. Usually this point coincides with the end of the dock. Then make a normal plait until you have reached the end of the sections of hair.*

F *Stitch along the length of the double plait so that it lies flat.*

G *The end result.*

BATHING TIPS

■ If you want to use warm water for bathing your horse but do not have access to hot water on site, leave buckets of water in the sun to warm up.

■ Cold water is much better for washing off horses after exercise in hot weather.

Now follow the steps below.

1 Wet your horse all over, taking care not to get water into his ears or eyes.

2 Apply the shampoo and work it into a lather, and clean the coat thoroughly. Take care around the horse's head and shield his eyes from the shampoo.

3 You can wash your horse's mane at the same time as his body, but it is easier to leave the tail until the body has been cleaned and rinsed.

4 Rinse the horse off thoroughly, using a sweat scraper to get rid of excess moisture.

5 If the weather is cool, dry the horse using towels. Another way is to put on an old but clean cotton-lined rug and pat it down so that the lining takes up the excess moisture.

6 Rug up according to the weather. Do not allow the horse to stand in the sun when his back is wet, as he could easily become burned.

7 To wash the tail, place it in a bucket of water (take care not to be kicked) and wet it thoroughly. Put down the bucket, add shampoo to the tail and work up a lather, cleaning the tail from top to bottom.

Using clean water, either in a bucket or from a hose, rinse the tail thoroughly. The bottom part can be whirled around to remove excess water.

REMEMBER

When you have bathed your horse, dry his heels very carefully to reduce the risk of cracked heels or mud fever developing.

Presentation

With your horse suitably trimmed and plaited, you can add the finishing touch to his appearance on the day with some judiciously applied quarter marks. These are intended to show off his hindquarters to best advantage, so if he is particularly weak behind do not draw attention to this fault by applying these marks. There are a number of stencils available which you place on the horse's quarters and then brush over to produce the required marks. However, the size of the stencil marks may not suit your particular horse, so it is as well to make the marks yourself.

Making quarter marks

Quarter marks are created by brushing or combing the coat in different directions to achieve a variety of shapes and effects. To give definition to the shapes, you should wet the hair – setting gel and hairspray also work wonders. Experimenting at home gives you the opportunity to decide which type of mark best suits your horse's

MAKING QUARTER MARKS

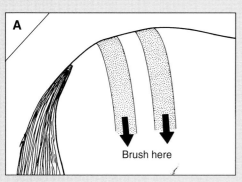

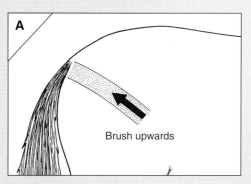

SQUARES Using a large body brush, make a couple of downward strokes from the top of the quarters.

SHARK'S TEETH Starting from a point about 10cm (4in) below the hip bone, brush diagonally upwards towards the tail.

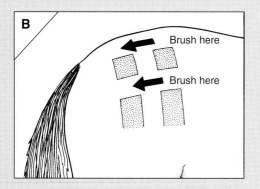

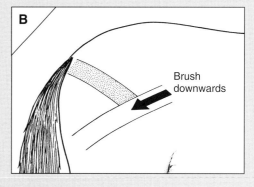

Return to the top of the quarters and brush in the direction of the coat. Now brush along the bottom of the downward marks to make the squares.

To make smaller squares, use a comb rather than a brush.

From the hip bone, make one downward brushing movement diagonally backwards.

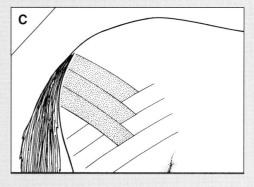

Repeat the upward and downward strokes until you have a line of 'teeth'.

hindquarters. The idea behind the marks is to make the quarters look stronger and symmetrical.

Squares may be large or small, while shark's teeth can be wide and short or long and narrow.

Start by brushing the horse's quarters in the direction of the coat then proceed as shown as opposite.

Make sure your pattern is symmetrical on each side of the horse's rump.

Training

You must train your horse at home so that he is fully prepared for the demands of his particular showing class.

In-hand

For in-hand classes, your horse must be taught to lead properly, as the judge does not want to see you messing about with an unruly animal.

A neat result. Whatever pattern you use, make sure it is symmetrical on each side of the horse's quarters.

Practise at home, remembering to walk at the horse's shoulder, and ensure that he walks out well, keeping his head straight. You must be able to control your horse and keep him walking and trotting straight. If you have to haul at him in order to slow down, the judge will not see the horse's best movement.

Your homework should also include standing up the horse for the judge. Although some breeds, such as the

Practise standing your horse up at home in readiness for inspection by the judge during a showing class.

Morgan, will have a particular stance, the judge basically needs to see the horse standing in balance, with his quarters neither trailing out behind nor tucked too far underneath. S/he will need to see all four legs, and when viewed from in front or behind the horse should be straight.

Ridden classes

Just as you would prepare for a dressage test by practising the movements, so you should prepare for your showing class by practising the various elements. Try to watch some of the top exponents of the art of showing at the larger shows and follow their example.

Schooling and manners

Horses in show classes should be well schooled and have perfect manners. If your horse is not ridden in company very often, make sure you get together with a group of friends and practise riding at all paces, so that you know he will behave in the presence of others in the show ring.

By working your horse in the company of others you will also discover whether he has a tendency to lash out, which can obviously be dangerous to other horses and riders. Equally, he should not try to take a chunk out of anyone walking around him: if the class demands that the horses are shown stripped (that is, with the saddle taken off) the judge will walk around them, so find out how your horse is likely to react by getting a friend to act as the judge while you stand him up for inspection.

Some showing classes require the judge to ride your horse, and the animal's manners will play an important part in his final placing. He should be trained to stand still while being mounted and dismounted, and should not move off until asked. The judge will not want to haul on the reins in order to stop, so ensure your horse will halt readily and stand still. He should also be used to strangers riding him.

TIP

Accustom your horse to being mounted from the ground *and* to having a rider legged up on to him, because the judge may do either.

Individual show and run-up

Keep your individual show to things that your horse does well – you are aiming to show control, rhythm, balance and obedience. You will need to show all the paces, but do not spend a lot of time in your horse's worst one. Ensure that all your transitions are smooth. If you use a figure-of-eight or circles, make sure that they are the proper shape – no square circles, please! Hacks and riding horses often need to show a rein back; four steps is enough, but these must be executed in a straight line and without a fight. Finally, keep your show short – an experienced judge can assess a horse very quickly.

Practise standing up your horse for the judge. The walking- and trotting-up procedure should also be perfected at home before venturing into the show ring.

Galloping and jumping

Working hunters and cobs are required to gallop in the show ring, and you will need to be brave enough to show off your horse to the best of his ability. Practise by asking your horse to gallop and then getting him to come back to

*Narrow fences
may feature in
working hunter
classes.*

you, and ensure that you are proficient on both reins.

For the jumping phase of a working hunter class you will need to aim at a fluent clear round, jumped from a good hunting pace. You may meet ditches, water trays or stiles, so practise these in schooling sessions before venturing into the show ring.

SHOW TACK

Bridles

There is now such a huge variety of in-hand bridles and headcollars that it is worth attending a large show to find out what the winners are wearing. If in doubt, go for something plainer: after all, the judge wants to see your horse and judge *him*, not the tack!

Each breed class has its own type of in-hand bridle, headcollar or halter, so check with the relevant society for the latest information. For ridden classes, decorative stitching is suitable for riding horse, hack and show pony classes, with coloured browbands for hacks and show ponies. Wide, plain cavesson nosebands are suitable for hunters and cobs (a wide noseband and browband can have the effect of shortening a long head), while narrow, stitched ones look good on ponies.

PREPARATION CHECKLIST

Before you enter a show class, you must be able to:

- Control your horse at all paces in company.

- Gallop and bring him back easily.

- Trot him up for the judge competently.

- Stand him up so that the judge can assess his conformation.

- Ensure that your horse will stand still while in line.

- Ensure that he will stand still while a rider mounts and dismounts.

- Execute an individual show effectively.

- Lead your horse properly – do put in the work with a youngster to ensure that he is well prepared and you can control him.

- Jump the required variety of fences you are likely to meet in your particular class.

Saddles

Show saddles for all classes are designed to show off the horse's shoulder, so the flaps are cut very straight. The saddle must suit the horse and rider and be comfortable, especially if the judge is to ride. Leather girths should be used for hunters, cobs and riding horses, but hacks and ponies can wear white webbing girths. Make sure that your leathers and irons are suitable for the judge – if you are small, take a spare set for the judge to use if necessary.

TIP

If you use a numnah, it will need to blend in with the colour of your horse's coat.

RINGCRAFT

Once you are actually in the ring, there are a number of points to bear in mind to maximize your chances of success.

- If your horse is the best-looking one in the class, have the confidence to go into the ring first.
- Conversely, try to avoid being near the most eye-catching horse in the field.
- Make the best possible use of the space, utilizing the corners.
- When you first enter the ring, make a check of the ground on the first circuit in case there are any problem areas to be avoided at faster paces. Studs may be worn.
- Try not to get into a bunch with other competitors – circle away discreetly to make more room for yourself.
- Be aware of other riders – inexperienced or unsporting competitors may get in front of you just as you are going past the judge.
- Check where the judge is looking – you then know where you have to show your horse off.
- Ride sensibly. This means not getting too close to other horses, keeping clear of those that are misbehaving, and trying to avoid being overtaken if you have to gallop, as your horse may become upset.
- Make use of the corners before and after the long side down which you gallop.
- Keep your individual show sharp and short. It should be designed to show off your horse's training but be flexible, as the judge may tell you what to do rather than let you perform your own version. S/he wants to see a good performance straightaway, so don't waste time riding aimlessly around. Show off your horse's paces and only attempt movements such as rein back if the execution is guaranteed to be very good.
- If you have to strip your horse and trot him up for the judge, be ready to walk up when it is your turn. Stand in front of the horse while the judge looks around him – ensure your reins do not drag on the ground. If you are asked any questions, answer them briefly and politely – the judge does not want the horse's entire life history! When you trot back towards the judge, carry on past, close enough for him/her to see the horse's action but not so close that s/he is in danger of being knocked over.
- Watch the judge and/or steward out of

ACTION POINTS

- Try to attend shows at various levels and watch the classes in which you are interested. There are many tips to be picked up, particularly by watching the professionals. Note how they use the ring, present their horses, and their attitude to the stewards and judges. If possible, watch them in the warming-up area and around their lorries, to see how the grooms prepare the horses.

- Check each show schedule carefully, as the rules may vary from show to show.

- Pay attention to detail *all* the time, and remember that your own determination to do well and to learn from each experience will pay dividends.

- Ensure that your horse is fully prepared for his class. If you are in any doubt, wait. Once you overface and worry your horse it will take that much longer to get him back on schedule.

- Keep a diary of your shows, including details such as how long it took you to get to the showground, ring conditions and the comments (and names) of the judges. Make observations on your performance, including areas where you feel you need to improve. As your season progresses, you should see yourself and your horse progressing too. You can also use your diary to plan your next season.

SUMMARY

- Treat your first year in showing as a learning experience. Take notice of what other competitors do – especially the successful ones!

- When making entries, it is sensible to take photocopies of your completed entry form, in case when you arrive at the show you find that your original entry was not received.

- Remember that you are competing to enjoy yourself, so whatever happens, smile – and put your negative days down to experience. There is an opportunity to learn in everything we do, especially with horses.

- If you insist on good manners at home, your horse will be well prepared for the show ring. Show horses do have to stand around, and a fidgety one is a nuisance for all concerned. A horse who will stand quietly while being prepared at the lorry also makes for calmer nerves on the rider's part.

LATE ARRIVALS

If you are late for your class you will need to ask permission from the judge to enter the ring. If judging is already underway you may be refused. Accept this with good grace – it is your responsibility to get to your classes on time.

KNOW THE RULES

You should be aware of all the rules for your class. Check out any rule changes at the start of the season to avoid embarrassment.

the corner of your eye so that you know immediately if you are asked to join the line-up.

AT THE END OF THE DAY

Whatever the result of your class, it is not acceptable to be rude to judges, stewards and officials, or any bystander. There is always another day and another show: the best way for you to learn is to ask the judge politely how you might improve on your performance in the future.

SEVEN

Dressage

Once regarded with trepidation by many competitors, dressage has grown considerably in popularity in recent years, attracting converts from all age groups.

Dressage has always consisted simply of walk, trot and canter, performed in a series of movements linked together to form a dressage 'test'. In fact, every rider does 'dressage' every day, yet, as those who pursue this equestrian art know, it is not quite so simple and straightforward as it may seem. Top riders like Nicole Uphoff make dressage appear easy and effortless, but many years of work have gone into training a horse – and rider – to such a high level.

Indeed, to become such a rider requires years of dedication and application, riding many, many horses of all standards. For those keen to pursue a competitive career in dressage, it is vital to have regular instruction. An experienced instructor who can guide you and your horse through the various levels is a great bonus. At the same time, being able to ride horses who are already established in their training and work will give you as a rider the chance to feel just what a shoulder-in or half-pass or flying change should be like. Once you know exactly what you are aiming for, it is easier to know whether or not you are on the right track.

DRESSAGE FOR ALL

Dressage is for everyone. No matter which equestrian discipline you wish to pursue, dressage is the foundation for everything. This is because dressage – or schooling – produces a horse which is supple, strong, obedient and well developed. As his training progresses, so the horse's muscles are built up and his self-carriage develops.

Just as the horse's body strengthens and learns to cope with the different demands made upon it, so must the rider's. Your balance and co-ordination will improve if you work at it, and your understanding of the aids and their application, and of how your horse moves, will all be increased.

A WILLING PARTNER

Dressage training is a progressive programme, but in order to keep your horse fresh you should include other work such as hacking, hill work and gymnastic jumping. If you spend all your time schooling, your horse may become sour – and an unwilling worker is an unhappy one. In order to get the best from your horse he must work *with* you, not against you, which means that you should never try to dominate him. Horses are not

Lungeing a horse has several benefits: to get the sting out of a particularly fresh horse before riding it; to exercise a horse who for some reason cannot be ridden; to assist in the training of a young horse; and to encourage any horse to work in an outline.

machines: they have feelings and 'off' days too. Recognize this and use it in your training; and if you are in a bad mood, tense or stressed, leave riding for another day – you can always work the horse from the ground on the lunge or long reins instead.

SCHOOLING

At the start of any schooling session, and at dressage competitions, it is important that you spend some time warming up your horse before asking him to undertake any serious work (see page 28). The aim is to get the horse working forwards rhythmically and obediently, with a swinging back. Your horse's age and stage of training will have an effect on how quickly he is loosened up and ready to work. In cold weather both horse and rider will take longer to warm up; the horse will also need a longer loosening-up period if he is tense, nervous or

perhaps stiff after a strenuous workout on the previous day.

End each schooling session with another 10 minutes at walk to allow the horse to relax, both physically and mentally.

The basics

Before aiming at the giddy heights of half-pass, canter pirouettes or piaffe, you must first get to grips with the foundations: your horse must move forward obediently, work in an acceptable outline for his level of training and in a good rhythm, and be supple, submissive and straight.

Straightness

Crookedness is one of the first problems that many riders encounter in their horses, but the fault can often be traced back to themselves – how can the horse move straight if the rider is sitting crookedly? So, whenever you ride, start off with a check of your riding position (see pages 23–24). You should review

Straightness is one of the first priorities. However, the horse cannot move straight if the rider's position is lacking in any way, so an important part of any schooling session is the rider's self-discipline to check and correct her riding position constantly.

your position constantly as you ride, making minor adjustments as necessary, with the aim of conforming to the ideal position as this enables the horse to carry his rider as efficiently as possible.

Obedience

It is important that your horse is obedient and responds immediately an aid is applied – this is known as 'being in front of the rider's leg'. If your horse is tardy, then he must be reminded: do not just apply a stronger aid or you will desensitize him. If he does not move forward when you apply the leg aids, back them up with a tap from your schooling whip. This is far kinder than banging your legs against the horse's sides.

Suppleness

The only way a horse can become supple is if his rider works him in a progressive training programme which develops his physique and paces. Using exercises such as loops, serpentines, circles of various sizes, spiralling in and out of circles, and lateral work (moving the horse sideways and forwards at the same time) will all help to improve his suppleness. All horses have a stiffer side, but it is important that you work both sides of your horse even though you may find one rein particularly difficult.

Free forward movement

At all times, ensure that your horse goes forward. He should work from behind (think of the hindquarters as the engine), with his hindlegs stepping well under his body, into a secure contact offered by the rider's hand.

There should be no tension through the horse's back and neck, and he should accept the rein contact without resistance.

This horse has dropped behind the contact: the rider needs to ride him forward and encourage him to take up the contact.

The outline of the horse will vary according to his stage of training.

Reaching your goals

Achieving all this is not so easy, and this is where it is vital you have someone on the ground to help. Regular lessons with a good instructor will set you on the right path, for each horse has his own problems and there is no single way which will work with every one. Sometimes you will have to try several different approaches in order to reach a particular goal. Throughout your schooling, there are several points to remember:

- Stay calm. If you tense up, this will be felt by the horse and matters will only become worse. Work through problems logically rather than giving in to fits of pique or temper.
- Remember that the horse learns through repetition. It is up to you to ensure that the lessons you are trying to teach are good lessons, because your horse will learn bad habits through repetition just as well as he will learn good habits. Be consistent in what you are asking your horse to do.
- Think about your horse's responses. Can he understand what you are asking? Could you make it clearer or easier for him? Is he fit enough (mentally as well as physically) to cope with the task you are setting him? Is he exhibiting resistance through pain or disobedience?
- Give your horse frequent rest periods at a free walk. These can also be used as a reward and relaxation when he has tried something new.
- Always let your horse know when he has done well.

A GOOD WALK

In a good walk, the horse should:

- Cover a lot of ground.
- Overtrack – that is, the hind feet should step well beyond the prints left by the forefeet.
- Move freely from the shoulder.
- Make his steps with a clear four-beat rhythm.

The walk is a pace which can only be improved a little through training.

A GOOD TROT

A good trot has:

- A clear two-beat footfall, as the horse springs from one diagonal pair of legs to the other, with a moment of suspension in between.
- Plenty of impulsion from behind, with the hind legs stepping under the body so that they step into the prints made by the forefeet.
- A rhythm which remains the same whether the rider is asking for a collected or a working trot.

The trot is the easiest gait for a horse, because at any one time he has two feet on the ground and so can balance and carry himself with less effort. It can be improved with training, because as the horse learns to take more weight on his hindquarters the shoulders are freed and the pace itself becomes freer and more expressive.

A GOOD CANTER

A good canter:

■ Is round and 'uphill', so that you feel as if you have plenty of horse in front of you.

■ Has a clear three-beat rhythm, with a moment of suspension.

■ Is well balanced.

If your horse has a poor canter there is only so much improvement to be made through training. Plenty of transitions will be more useful than simply cantering round and round.

DRESSAGE COMPETITIONS

Each country has its own progressive series of dressage tests. Some are used exclusively in pure dressage competitions, others as the first phase in a horse trial.

Your national dressage organization should be able to supply you with copies of their recognized tests. It is extremely helpful to have these before you even start competing, as they can be used in planning your schooling programme.

Once your schooling is progressing well, you can begin to think about preparing for your first competition.

PLANNING A PROGRAMME

Let's take the example of a rider who wants to compete in one-day events. She needs to gain competitive experience in the dressage arena, so she plans to enter a number of local dressage competitions at the lower levels.

Studying test sheets

Before our rider can plan her training schedule, she needs to know what the tests at these levels entail. By obtaining copies of all the relevant test sheets she can examine the various requirements.

On the back of the sheets there is a section which lays down the standards expected of horse and rider. Comparing these for the Preliminary and Novice

BELOW
The dressage arena.

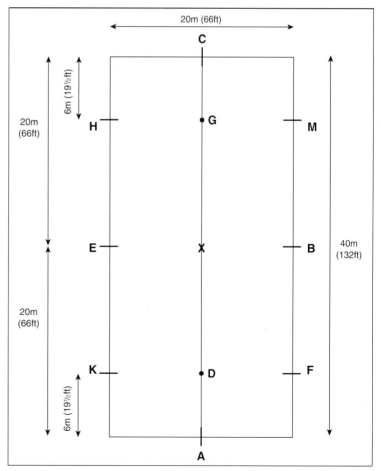

Mark out an arena in a corner of your field in which to work. You can accustom the horse to working within the confines of an arena, and it is also the only way to judge whether or not you are performing the dressage test movements accurately.

levels, our rider notes that in the Preliminary tests the horse is expected to 'move freely forward without collection but with active hindquarters', while at Novice level this has progressed to 'moves freely forward without collection but showing a slightly greater degree of engagement than that required at Preliminary level'. She then examines all the movements and paces required for each test.

Finally, the rider notes that some of the tests are ridden in a 20 x 40m arena and some in a 20 x 60m arena. She therefore determines to spend time practising in arenas of both dimensions in order to be confident about performing in either area.

Ridden work

The next step is for our rider to work through the movements required in the tests, so that she is absolutely clear about the aids she needs to apply for each one and how to execute it accurately in the arena. Her plan is to:

- Make sure first of all that her schooling area is marked out accurately.
- Set specific goals for each schooling session to ensure that she practises all of the required movements and paces. It can be tempting to stick to the things you find easy and know you can do well, and neglect the trickier school movements.
- Seek assistance from an instructor who can watch her riding through various tests and provide pointers on accuracy and the quality of the movements.
- Incorporate some of the movements – such as halts, free walk on a long rein, and upward and downward transitions

– into her roadwork and hacks. This will help combat boredom and give an added purpose to hacking.

By working through the requirements in this way and seeking help from an instructor, our rider is able to work out a date for her first competition, based on when she and her horse will be able to give a good account of themselves.

COMPETING

Preparation

In the run-up to a dressage competition, implement the following:

- Work out a warming-up plan to use when you practise at home and on the competition day.
- Learn your dressage test thoroughly well in advance of the competition day.
- Use the movements in the tests at the level at which you are working as part of your schooling sessions.
- Try to be accurate whenever you ride movements: getting into the habit at home will mean that it is second nature in competitions.
- Practise in a 20 x 40m arena, or a 20 x 60m arena if you are working at the higher levels. This ensures that you will be familiar with the dimensions and so can produce a more accurate test. If you always work in a larger area, you may find it difficult to cope in a standard arena.
- Practise on grass arenas as well as on indoor and outdoor school surfaces.

Entering a competition

It is a sensible policy to enter smaller competitions first, rather than plunging straight in at the deep end. Local riding clubs and centres often hold small dressage competitions; the schedule will indicate which tests are being used and any conditions that apply – for example, there may be classes which are open only to horse-and-rider combinations which have not been placed in a dressage competition.

Pre-entries are always required for dressage competitions: this allows the secretary to work out timings in advance of the day itself. The schedule will advise you who to contact for your time(s); these are normally given out a day or two in advance of the event.

At the competition

The time you have been given will be the time you actually start your test – in practice, you will need to be in the warm-up area earlier so that the ring steward knows you are there and can look over your tack. You should check that everything is running to time, as this may affect your warm-up.

Your work at home should have given you an idea of how long you will need for warming up. If your horse starts to tense up, resist the temptation to niggle away at him. Take him to a quiet corner of the showground and carry on with your usual warming-up procedure. Try not to tense up yourself, as this will inevitably be transmitted to the horse. Remember that the work you are doing is what you do every day, so there is no need to worry!

Occasionally a competitor withdraws from the competition on the day. If they are before you in the order, you may be able to ride your test earlier. If your horse is ready and you wish to go in earlier

A neatly turned out young rider and pony warming up for a dressage competition.

TIP

If you warm up your horse in protective boots, ask your helper or the steward to remove them before you enter the arena. A whip is fine in the practice area, but hand it to your helper before going in for your test.

then do so, but if you are not fully prepared there is no obligation on you to take an earlier time.

As the previous competitor finishes their test, you will be called by the steward. Leave the warm-up area and make your way to the arena. At some events you will have to ride over to the judge's car to give your number, but usually it is enough just to ride past so that the judge's writer can see your number. Take this time to walk and trot around the arena to accustom your horse to the arena boards. Do not enter the arena until you hear the signal

from the judge – usually their car horn. If you do enter before the signal you will be eliminated.

Take a deep breath, relax and enter the arena, looking towards the judge's car (which is usually parked at C). As you salute, remember to smile – you are meant to enjoy this!

TIP

Accustom your horse to arena marker boards before the competition to avoid spookiness on the day.

You should know the test well enough for you to be able to concentrate on riding and getting the best from your horse. If you make a mistake, it is not the end of the world: it just means that your marks for that particular movement will not be as good as you had hoped.

If you go wrong – or forget the test

ACTION POINTS

■ Take your horse's individuality into account when preparing his work programme. For example, if he warms up better in canter than in trot, introduce this pace earlier on.

■ Aim at the subtlest aids you can – your horse should go forwards immediately you ask. Riding should not be a huge effort for the rider, and carrying the rider should not be a difficult task for the horse.

■ Do not underestimate or under-use

transitions. They are extremely useful as a means of getting the horse in front of the leg and engaging the hindquarters.

■ If you find yourself getting nowhere fast, seek help from an experienced instructor. Everyone hits a plateau in their riding or schooling at some point, but problems can always be overcome. The only block to your riding progress is in your mind.

completely – come back to a walk, then halt. Relax, and, if you can recall the test, restart where you need to. Judges are not monsters and will often put you back on the right track if you are completely overcome by nerves. Of course, errors will be penalized, and if you go wrong on three occasions in the same test you will be eliminated.

A dressage test lasts for just a few minutes and you have done all the movements many times over at home, so do not feel that it is a great problem putting it all together for a competition. If your horse gets very tense you will need to ride him sympathetically – fits of temper on your part will not be appreciated.

Do remember to leave the arena at walk on a loose rein – your test is not over until you have done so.

After the competition

Whether things have gone well or badly on the day, remember that dressage tests are simply opportunities for you to measure the progress of your horse's education, so after each competition do make use of the judge's marks and comments to implement constructive changes in your horse's schooling.

SUMMARY

■ Work on your riding position constantly – it has an incredible effect on the horse's way of going.

■ Before you try to teach your horse anything, you must be clear about what you are trying to achieve.

■ Always give your horse time to understand what you are asking him to do.

■ Educating your horse will take not days, weeks or months, but *years*.

EIGHT

Showjumping

Most people and horses can learn to jump single fences, whether they be uprights or spreads, in good style, but the real skill comes in jumping a course, with both horse and rider staying in balance, jumping in good style and producing a fluent, accurate, polished round. To be successful in showjumping you need to jump good, clear rounds consistently and have the knowledge to take the shortest route but still jump rounds without faults when the pressure is on during a jump-off.

The rider must make it easy for her horse to jump: it is up to you to produce a good-quality canter with your horse's hindlegs coming well under his body, while you maintain a good contact and

A confident partnership. The pony is jumping very neatly and the rider is looking ahead and riding her track as a whole, not as individual jumps.

Going forward before the horse has taken off can result in the rider effectively ceasing to drive the horse on, and can produce a refusal.

stay in balance with the horse. It is the horse's job to jump. Whether the horse jumps off a long stride or puts in a short one, you should be unperturbed – you must still be there, helping the horse by keeping your legs on and riding into a good contact, so that the horse's job remains easy. If you fail to keep the contact and throw your hands away, you are effectively throwing away the impulsion and the horse will be unable to jump properly.

The first few times you 'drop' the horse he may still try to jump for you, but if you consistently let him down he will soon start refusing to jump altogether. Refusals and run-outs are generally the rider's fault.

A horse will refuse to jump because:

- He is in pain, perhaps due to the onset of a health problem, or because every time he jumps he receives a jab in the mouth from his rider or she thumps back into the saddle, jarring his back.
- He is unable to do what you ask because he has not been prepared properly in terms of his education and training, and is being overfaced or scared.
- He is unable to do what you ask because you have made a poor approach to the fence and given the horse an impossible task.
- He is unsure what his rider wants; for example, the rider stops telling the horse to go (that is, rider's legs freeze on the approach) or she drops the contact on the approach.

Working over poles at home as a preliminary to jumping.

- Some horses genuinely do not want to jump, but often this can be traced back to a problem with a previous rider.

Run-outs are caused by the rider 99 per cent of the time, because she has:

- Failed to approach the fence properly, so asking the horse a question which he cannot answer.
- Failed to ride the horse, so that he is left without any instructions.
- Pulled the horse out herself, as she is worried about the fence.

BENEFITS OF GRIDWORK

One of the best ways to learn to ride your horse effectively is to undertake gridwork exercises. A 'grid' consists of a sequence of fences, either in a line or set out in the shape of a box, a figure-of-eight or other combination. The various grids address different horse and rider problems, but they are all invaluable in teaching the rider balance, control, co-ordination of the aids and accuracy.

RIDING A COURSE

Whether you are putting two or three fences together or riding a proper course of ten fences or so, the objective is the same: keep the quality of the canter, keep the rhythm and let the fences come to you. If you start looking for strides and fiddling with the reins on the approach to

Different types of
showjumping fence.

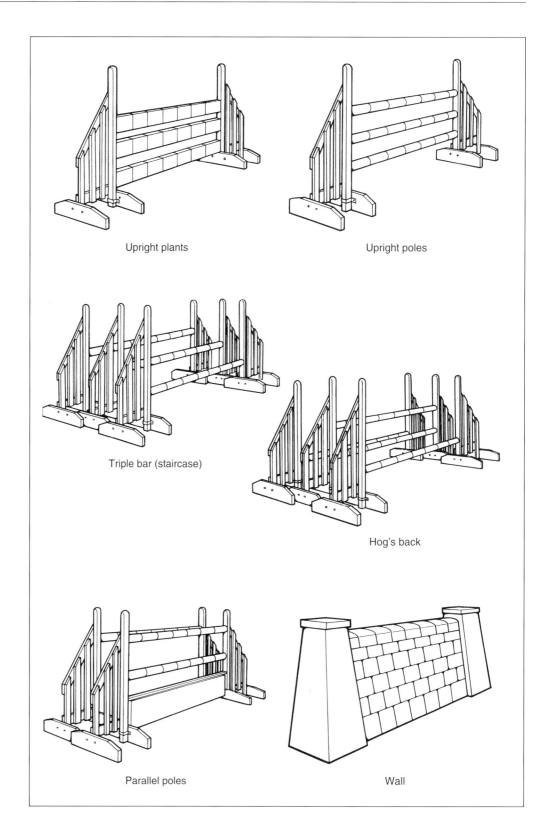

Upright plants

Upright poles

Triple bar (staircase)

Hog's back

Parallel poles

Wall

Introducing a young horse to jumping fillers, which have been placed at the sides of the fence – the crosspole is used to encourage the horse to jump in the middle of the fence. As he becomes accustomed to the fillers they are closed in, until the horse is jumping over them.

A youngster showing his greenness as he gives this tiny wall plenty of air. At this stage it is important that he goes forward willingly – which this gelding certainly does.

Jumping bigger fences tests the rider's balance.

the jumps you will disturb your horse's rhythm and balance. If you are unable to approach a fence without your horse getting excited and speeding up, then you need to work more on his flatwork and gymnastic jumping exercises. You should aim for a sensible, controlled round, in a consistent rhythm. Remember to ride the course as a whole, not as a series of separate parts, although each individual fence will require a slightly different approach depending on whether it is an upright or spread, part of a combination, and so on. Similar principles apply as for jumping the different types of fence across country (see pages 124–128).

COMPETING AT A SHOW

When you feel confident about jumping courses at home and have tried out a few jump-off techniques, it is time to think about going to a show. The show schedule should give you an idea of the fence height and conditions for each class, for example: 'First Novice – 75cm (2ft 6in) for horse/pony and rider combinations which have never been placed in a jumping competition'.

Most shows also run 'minimus' or 'clear round' classes. These are not competitive: you simply go in and jump the course, and rosettes are awarded to all those who jump clear. Sometimes the height of the course is raised throughout the day. These are also called 'training' or 'schooling' classes in some schedules.

If you are happily jumping 90cm (3ft) courses at home, then enter 75cm (2ft 6in) and 84cm (2ft 9in) classes at shows. It always pays to be better prepared than your class demands in order to make allowance for factors like competition nerves.

When walking the course prior to your round, try to determine which fences may cause your horse to be spooky or nappy. You will need to ride with even greater determination than normal!

Walking the course

There are a number of points to bear in mind when walking a showjumping course:

- Take note of the ring entrance in relation to the collecting ring/warming-up area. Will your horse leave other horses readily? It is not unknown for people to have their horses led up to the ring entrance.
- Does the course have a separate entry and exit point? Will you have enough space to pull up once you have negotiated the last fence? If space is tight, decide where you are going to go.
- Where are the judges situated? You may need to ride past them so that they can see your number.
- Where is the start and finish of the timing apparatus? I have seen people eliminated because they failed to cross

the start line – they had not noticed that it was some way back from the first fence and they came in short to the first obstacle.

- Is there any particular fence that you want to trot/canter past as you wait for the bell to go for the start of your round? Make sure you go past it as soon as you enter the ring, as some judges ring the bell very quickly and you have only a limited time (usually 60 seconds) in which to commence your round.
- Note the position of the first fence: is it towards or away from the collecting ring? If it is going away, you will probably have to ride even more positively to avoid your horse backing off and trying to stay with the others.
- Walk the line you intend to ride between each fence, ensuring that you will be giving your horse every chance

1 *Fences on a showjumping course are often set at related distances, with a certain number of strides between the obstacles, even though the fences are not doubles or trebles. Here the rider is landing over one fence and is already sighting on the next one, which is five strides away.*

2 *On the stride after landing the rider is still inclined forward, but is looking ahead.*

3 *Now she has raised her upper body, as she balances her horse and maintains the activity of his hindquarters. The rider is trying to keep an evenness of stride and still looks ahead as she nears the next obstacle.*

4 *The horse clears the fence, although the rider has gone forward rather too much. Note how the horse's body posture mirrors that of the rider.*

Walk the course at a competition on your own or with your trainer if possible. Do not be tempted to chat with your friends or you will miss the opportunity to learn a great deal about the course. When waiting to jump, do not watch other riders if this is likely to affect your nerves – if you are a sensitive, nervous competitor, seeing others crash into fences or stop through silly mistakes is not conducive to a good round.

to jump. There is no point in cutting corners during the first round, so make the best possible use of the arena.

- There will not always be straight lines between fences, so consider how you will ride dog-legs and other odd lines to give you a good approach to the next fence.

- Note where there is a long gap between fences and determine not to let your horse become strung out and flat. Keep him together with his hindquarters operating properly and he will be able to jump better.

- Check the distances within combinations. These should be fairly standard, but your horse's stride may be shorter or longer than average and you will have to cope by either holding him together for shorter strides or pushing him on for longer ones. A horse's stride is about 3.6m (12ft), so if you practise pacing out 90cm (3ft) you can work out how many of your strides

equate to one stride of your horse.

- It is easy to lose impulsion when you have to come around a corner to a fence, so allow for this and ensure that you are always creating enough impulsion.

- Make sure you cross the finishing line.

- On completion of your course walk, go over the course in your head. Remember it by fence colour or jump type, whichever method suits you best.

Warming up

Before you start warming up, check the start board near the entrance to your jumping ring. This is where you put your number down to ensure your place in the jumping order. The ring steward will call you when the rider before you goes in, but it is up to you to keep your eye on proceedings so that you can time your warm-up and be ready to jump when it is your turn.

Collecting rings at shows can be

Start your practice over a cross pole and then an upright, working up to a spread and then a parallel to get you and your horse operating properly.

extremely busy places, so you will need to have your wits about you. The rule for working-in arenas – pass left hand to left hand – should be second nature to every rider – but unfortunately this is not always the case, so when riding in do make sure that you look ahead and are aware of other riders.

Warm up on the flat first in walk, trot and canter, making use of transitions, the objective being to get your horse loosened up and listening to you.

It is useful if you have a helper with you who can take charge of the practice fence, otherwise you will have to rely on other riders' helpers or keep getting off to adjust the fence. When you are ready to jump, make your first practice fence a cross pole. Pop over this a couple of times, then make the fence into an upright.

Once you are happy with your horse's and your performance over this, make the fence into a spread. You will get to know how much jumping your horse needs before it goes in the ring, but be careful that you do not do too much and leave your best jumping in the collecting ring!

Initially the practice fences may be useful as much for settling your nerves as for warming up your horse. If you are worried about competing, then go in the minimus or clear round class first.

In the ring

Once you enter the ring for your round, bear in mind all the points you noticed when you walked the course. Concentrate on the job in hand and listen for the bell to tell you that you may start your round. If you make a mistake, get yourself together – stop if necessary – and then re-present your horse at the fence. Do not look back if you hear your horse rattle a pole: look ahead to the next jump, because that is the one you can do something about.

RIDING INDOOR COURSES

Practising jump-off turns during an indoor schooling session.

■ Indoor jumping courses are usually tighter on space than outdoor ones, so you must have a supple, obedient horse. As always, this is achieved through flatwork and gymnastic jumping exercises.

■ The onus is on you, the rider, to use your aids effectively so that your horse is balanced around corners, makes full use of the arena, is in a good rhythm and so on.

■ With indoor courses the fences tend to be upon you quite quickly, so it is even more important that you look ahead and know exactly where you want to go. Dithering about will result in run-outs or refusals.

Jump-off courses

If you jump clear and get through to the jump-off, find out what the shortened course will be. At the larger events the course details are generally posted near the ring entrance and will include the jump-off fences. At smaller shows you may find that the jump-off does not necessarily follow the original numerical order.

Take the time to look at the jump-off course from all sides of the ring so that you can work out the quickest route. Jump-offs are not won by screeching round as if you are in the Monaco Grand Prix. The secret lies in taking out strides, keeping a good rhythm and, of course, jumping clear. If you try to go too fast you will make your horse jump flatter and will run the risk of knocking down fences. If possible, watch other competitors jumping the course before you go in. You will then be able to see if anyone else is trying your jump-off route and if any problems are becoming apparent.

You should practise jump-off techniques at home before trying them under the spotlight of competition. When you are competing, it is easy to fall back into bad habits like throwing away the rein and forgetting to use your legs, so it is best to have the correct way of riding so ingrained that even under the pressure of competition you do the best for your horse.

Whatever happens...

Take time after the show to reflect on the day. Consider your pre-show preparation,

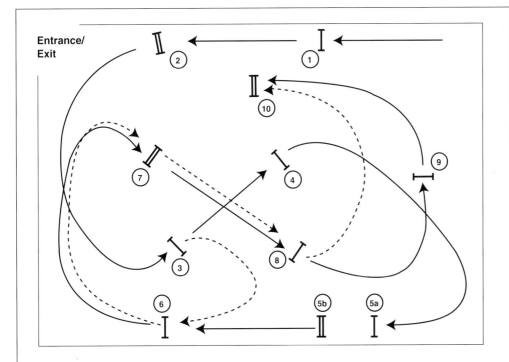

Direction of first round ⟶

Jump off - - - - - ➤

This jump-off course uses fences 3, 6, 7, 8 and 10 from the original course.

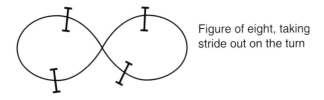

Figure of eight, taking stride out on the turn

Jumping a fence at an angle to give a good line to the next obstacle

Practising jump-off techniques.

In a jump-off, when turns are important, you should plan your line carefully and make use of redundant fences to help you turn. This rider is using the fence to help her achieve a tight right-hand turn back to the next fence.

ACTION POINTS

■ After a show, run over the day's events and work out what can be improved.

■ Devise a plan of action to deal with any problems which may have arisen and prevent them occurring at your next competition.

SUMMARY

■ Carry out your homework thoroughly before competing at a show.

■ Enter classes where the jumps are smaller than you are jumping at home – then you and your horse will feel confident.

■ Work out your jump-off route and be committed to it – any indecision will have an adverse effect on your performance.

■ If you make a mistake, stay calm and get on with the rest of the course.

what happened on the day and what you can do to improve things next time. Try not to get bogged down in pessimistic mutterings if you had an unsuccessful show. Imagine you were an impartial spectator watching your round – it was probably nowhere near as bad as it felt!

NINE

Hunter Trials and Cross Country

Riding and jumping across country, tackling hedges, ditches, water and many other hazards, is a very exciting part of competing. As the fences are solid and will not knock down, it is vital that both horse and rider are suitably prepared and confident. Both must be fit enough to cope with the demands of cross country competition: even 'low-key' courses will often be around 2.4km (1 $\frac{1}{2}$ miles) in length and, depending on the location, may be laid out over very hilly terrain. It is unfair to expect a tired horse to gallop and jump, but it is doubly unfair to expect him to cope with the burden of an exhausted, unbalanced rider.

In order to enjoy a cross country competition or hunter trial, you must be able to control your horse so that you can move on at a good pace in between fences, steady and balance up before jumping, keep the horse on an accurate line for difficult obstacles, bring the speed right down to negotiate jumps into 'space' or drop fences, ride positively at fences which are 'rider frighteners', and ride according to the feel your horse is giving you. In addition to the fitness and control, you must also have the technical knowledge, so that you know how to approach each fence to jump it in the safest way for you and your horse.

TEACHING YOUR HORSE TO JUMP FIXED FENCES

Before a horse starts to jump across country he should have been taught the basics of jumping via gridwork and small courses of showjumps. During this time you may pop him over small ditches and introduce him to walking in and out of water. Once the horse is happy and confident over 90cm (3ft) showjumps of all kinds, you can start to tackle fixed fences.

The horse's initial cross country sessions should be undertaken on a course where the fences are well built but small, as he needs to learn – without injuring himself – that these fences will not knock down if he touches them. Beware of schooling over flimsy cross country fences: do not think you are being kind to the horse in asking him to jump less solid fences. Solid ones are much more inviting to the horse and will result in a cleaner jump.

Start off over small logs or other uprights such as small post-and-rail fences or palisades. All the fences you will normally find at a competition can usually be found in miniature at training centres or cross country courses which are available for hire. Make sure that you include ditches, small steps (up and down) and water fences in your preparation.

It is worth checking the venues for the larger horse trials events, as schooling sessions are often available over these courses. The smaller fences on some of these would be a useful next step once your horse is jumping small (say 75cm/2ft 6in) solid fences happily. Clinics with top event riders are also held at various venues and are well worth attending. At these, you should also be able to get advice on a suitable pace for your horse across country, bearing in mind his current level of education.

Before you enter your first competition your horse should be going forward at a good canter in a good rhythm, tackling any fence happily. You must be able to control the speed, as you may want to bring him back to a trot for some fences. Initially, do not worry about going fast or jumping all the difficult alternatives. Your objective is to build confidence in both yourself and your horse.

A ... *Cross country riding requires commitment from the rider. Here the rider is approaching a drop with plenty of activity. She is resisting the temptation to pitch forward...*

B ... *resulting in a confident jump from the horse...*

C ... *with the rider leaning back to counteract the effect of the drop.*

An example of how the terrain can be used to make a fence more difficult. The land drops away on the approach to the fence and the rider has to maintain a very accurate line in order to jump it at the best place.

TIPS

■ When approaching a fence, you should feel that three-quarters of the horse is in front of you. This means that in effect you are sitting 'in behind' the horse and are ready to counteract any backward or negative tendencies he may exhibit. If you are in this position and the horse starts to back off the fence, you are in the best place to drive him forward.

■ Prepare the horse for the fence in time, but not so far in advance that you waste time. Around 100m (100yd) out from a fence should be adequate, and remember that the last three strides before a fence belong to the horse – so if you haven't got it right by four strides out, you probably won't get it right!

TACKLING CROSS COUNTRY FENCES

Upright   Horses generally find the upright fences more difficult to judge than spreads, so you should not approach too fast. Controlled impulsion is what is needed.

Parallel   Plenty of impulsion is required in order to jump a parallel fence, so that you approach on a strong, increasing stride.

Combination   Check out the distances in combinations carefully and determine the line you will take. You must allow the horse time to see what he has to do.

Bounce Approach this type of fence in a short, bouncy canter with plenty of impulsion. The strength of the pace will be dictated by the distance between and the make-up of the two elements: for example, if the second element is a wide spread more pace will be needed than if both elements are uprights. The horse must be kept together and round; beware of dropping the contact or failing to keep your leg on.

Trakehner This consists of a rail suspended over a ditch and a strong canter approach is needed, with the rider ready for the horse to shorten as he sees the ditch.

Ditch in front of or behind a fence A ditch in front of a fence will generally set up the horse for a decent jump – often the rider is more perturbed by a ditch than the horse is. You must approach with sufficient impulsion.

Hollow This type of fence used to be called a 'coffin'. Plenty of impulsion and

A *Horse and rider meet a hollow (coffin) fence for the first time. Although the rider has ridden very positively over the first element you can see how the horse is already backing off the second element – the ditch.*

B *Here the horse is saying 'Hang on, I don't like the look of this hole in the ground' ...*

C *... but the rider quickly re-establishes control and uses strong leg aids to encourage the horse over the fence.*

Cross country fences.

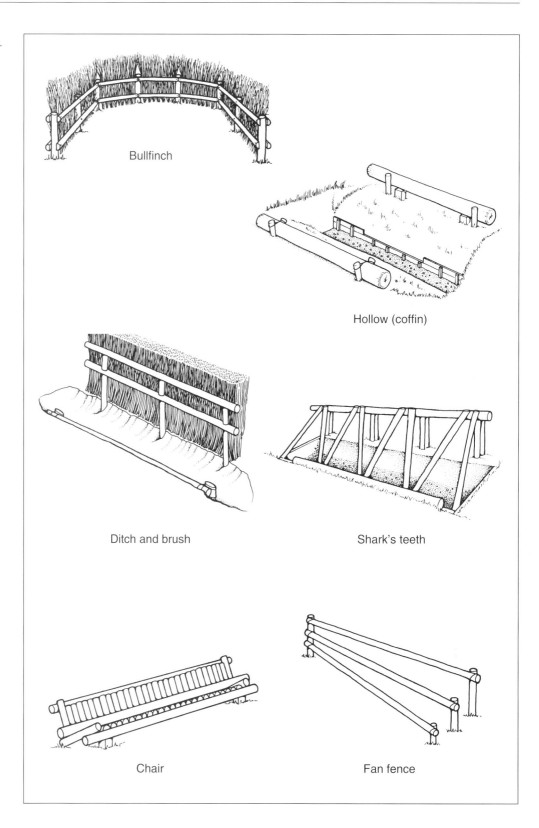

Bullfinch

Hollow (coffin)

Ditch and brush

Shark's teeth

Chair

Fan fence

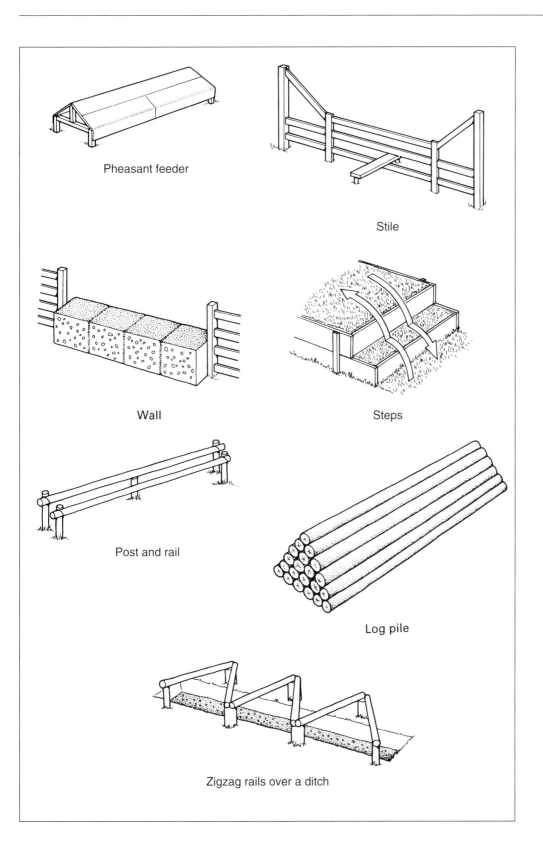

Pheasant feeder

Stile

Wall

Steps

Post and rail

Log pile

Zigzag rails over a ditch

a short, bouncy canter are required, and the horse needs time to see that it can land over the first part of the combination without ending up in the ditch. If the pace is slow you must keep plenty of leg on to maintain the impulsion.

Sunken road   Approach this fence in a similar way to a hollow.

Bullfinch   A strong, short stride is needed on the approach to this type of brush fence.

Bank   Approach with plenty of impulsion, with your horse's hindquarters well engaged.

Corner   It is vital to get your line right here. Divide the angle between the two rails and jump that imaginary line at right angles.

Drop   At a drop fence you want to encourage the horse to jump out rather than drop down too severely, so the approach needs to be on a lengthening stride but not too fast. If you shorten into

a drop, the trajectory on landing will be too steep.

Fence at the top of a downhill slope You do not want the horse to take off too far away at this type of fence, so approach in a bouncy, short-striding canter.

Fence at the bottom of a downhill slope   A bouncy and short-striding canter is again required, but it is preferable for the horse to stand off the fence.

Ski jump   Approach a ski jump in a slow trot, but as always, the slower the pace, the stronger the rider's legs need to be.

Steps   Jump steps down from a short, bouncy canter or from trot. Approach steps up in a strong, rounded canter – your horse's hindlegs must be well engaged or he will find each step up increasingly difficult.

Into water   Approach a fence into water in a slow but strong pace, ensuring that you hold your horse together. This also applies to jumping fences in water.

CROSS COUNTRY EQUIPMENT
Protective boots
It is sensible to protect your horse's legs from bruises and injuries by fitting him with boots for cross country schooling and competing.

Brushing boots are generally used all round; however, there are different thoughts on how much protection these should offer. Some people like to protect their horse's legs as much as possible, using boots which are extremely well padded; others use boots which will

Jumping a corner.

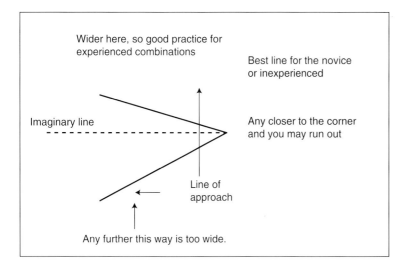

Wider here, so good practice for experienced combinations

Best line for the novice or inexperienced

Imaginary line

Any closer to the corner and you may run out

Line of approach

Any further this way is too wide.

protect but will also let the horse feel it if he hits something, the idea being that the horse will use himself better and pick up his feet more the next time.

Overreach boots may also be used. Again, some riders swear by them, while others feel that they can cause problems: for example, if they invert they offer no protection anyway, and there is the possibility that the horse might tread on the boots and interrupt the rhythm of his stride.

Boots or bandages?

Applying bandages correctly is an art, and one which many people cannot master. If done incorrectly, bandaging can damage your horse's legs so it is probably as well to stick to boots, which are simpler to apply. If you do use bandages:

- They must be applied over a protective layer, for example Porter boots or gamgee.
- The pressure must be the same all the way down.
- The bandages should not be applied so tightly as to limit blood circulation, nor so loosely that they slip down.

A *A bold, confident jump up the first step of a series.*

B *The horse's hindquarters have come well underneath him, providing the impulsive power for the next step. Gridwork helps to activate the horse's hindquarters in this way.*

C *Plenty of 'oomph' to tackle the final step up.*

- The tapes should be tied on the outside of the leg, never at the front on the bone or at the back on the tendon.
- The tapes should be sewn as well as tied.
- Adhesive tape, such as insulating tape, should be applied over the bandage tapes as extra insurance against their coming undone.
- When the bandages are removed, rub over the horse's legs briefly to restore circulation.

TIP

Insulating tape can also be used over boots to ensure that velcro-fastened boots are extra secure.

Knee boots

Skeleton knee boots may be used on young horses when schooling over fixed fences.

The boots consist of leather pads which cover the knee and are held in place with straps above and below. The top strap must be tight enough to prevent the boot slipping down, while the bottom strap should be fitted so that when the horse's leg is bent, there is enough room between the strap and the back of the knee to allow for the flexion of the joint.

Skeleton knee boots or caps differ from the knee boots used for travelling in that they do not have any felt material around the knee pad itself.

Tack

- The bridle you use for cross country work should be made from a reasonably wide and heavy leather, as the strains placed upon it when travelling across country can be great.
- Your bridle must be in good order, with the stitching, hooks and billets intact.
- Rubber-covered reins provide better grip.

USING BOOTS

- Use four-strap boots on the front and five-strap on the hindlegs. If you use five-strap boots on the front you will find that they are too long and will interfere with the knee joint.

- All straps should face backwards.

- Ensure that the pressure of the straps is even.

- Felt-type boots are not suitable for hard work, as they offer minimal protection and will stretch with use.

- Boots with sheepskin linings will become heavy once the horse has been in water.

- Keep all boots clean – using dirty boots on your horse will result in rubs and sores.

- If sports medicine boots are used they must be the correct size for your horse (measured according to the amount of bone) and carefully fitted.

- Tie a knot in the end of your reins for added security in case they were to come undone at the buckle. A knot also makes it easier to gather up the reins if you have to slip them going over a drop fence.
- Your horse may be more difficult to control across country, so you should consider this when making your choice of bit.
- If you use a running martingale, rein stops are a must to prevent the martingale rings getting caught up in the rein buckles.
- A breastplate is advisable to prevent the saddle slipping back when jumping or galloping uphill.
- Your saddle should be a good fit for both horse and rider. A flatter cantle than is usual in a general-purpose or jumping saddle is advisable, as this will allow you to move your seat back – essential when jumping across country.
- Rawhide stirrup leathers are the strongest and are favoured by cross country riders.
- Heavy stirrup irons are preferable to light ones, as they will hang down and are easier to locate if your foot accidentally comes out of the iron.
- Leather girths such as Atherstone or Balding types are shaped to give extra room at the horse's elbow and prevent chafing. Leather is also stronger than synthetic materials.
- An overgirth or surcingle is essential as extra insurance in case your ordinary girth breaks. Use a couple of loops of elastic to keep the surcingle on top of the girth, otherwise it will slip back and may dig into the horse.
- A numnah is not necessary if your saddle fits properly, but many people

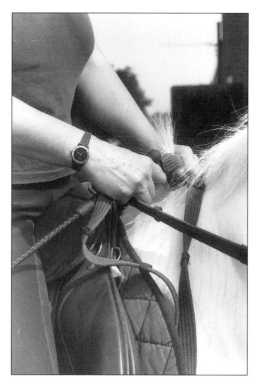

Bridging the reins – a handy technique if your horse tends to get strong and tries to pull the reins out of your hands.

like to use one for cross country riding to absorb the horse's sweat – a thin cotton one is useful for this.

AT THE COMPETITION

Walking the course

If you are inexperienced at cross country riding it is a good idea to walk the course with your instructor or a friend who is knowledgeable and experienced at cross country riding.

Remember that the first time your horse sees the course will be as he jumps it, so he is very reliant on you for instructions on where and how fast to go, and when and how to jump. You should make sure you know exactly where you are going, how you will tackle each fence and how it relates to the next, so that you know whether or not you will have to slow down.

Two combinations tackling a similar jump. Note the differences in both horses and riders – in the bottom picture the horse is more onward bound and the rider has compensated more for the drop down.

Whether it is your first, tenth or hundredth course, you must ride it positively, otherwise your horse will start to question you and worry about what is in front of him. This will lead to refusals or a poor jump at best, and possibly an accident.

An example

Let us take an imaginary course walk and talk through it.

The start is located close to where riders will be warming up, so it is quite natural that your horse may nap towards the warming-up area or be reluctant to leave it in the first place. You will therefore need to be positive and ready to deal with a backward-thinking horse.

Fence one is on a downward slope and is only a short distance from the start. It is an inviting brush fence, but still needs to be attacked because the horse may be thinking of his friends in the warm up area and it is important that you set the tone for the rest of the round. If you dribble down to the fence you are likely to have a stop.

The course now swings around to the right and the second fence is a log – again, a straightforward fence but one which needs to be met with plenty of impulsion. As yet, horse and rider are probably not in a consistent rhythm and dallying could produce a run-out or refusal.

Next comes a long gallop across a field to fence three, which is two steps down. While you can enjoy galloping, you must be able to slow down sufficiently to enable you to drop back into an active trot on the approach to the steps. You cannot afford for your horse to jump too boldly down steps, as he may overjump and miss the platform between each step – a recipe for disaster.

After the steps the course swings right again and heads for the next fence, a hedge. Natural fences such as hedges are easier to jump than 'island' fences (those stuck in the middle of fields) as it is easy for a horse to run out at an island fence, particularly if the rider's legs are weak or tired. There is a ditch in front of this hedge, so you must approach with plenty of impulsion to enable the horse to jump the spread. Too much of an 'up and down' jump will place you in danger of the horse 'losing a leg' in the ditch, although most will do their utmost to clear a ditch.

The next couple of jumps are relatively straightforward (a tiger trap and a post and rail), but then comes a water hazard: into the water over a small drop, over a small log in the water, and exit over another small log. Just as for an ordinary step, you need to throttle back and come into the fence in a strong, controlled trot. You do not want your horse to jump too fast into water, as the drag when he lands will be considerable. You also need to be in balance for the drop as the jump in the water and the fence out follow in quick succession. Impulsion (not speed) is required. Once you have mastered the art of jumping into water you may find it appropriate to come into some fences in canter, but again it is controlled impulsion which is the secret to success.

Once out of the water the course heads uphill, then turns left to straighten up for the next fence, an elephant trap. It is important that you do not lose the engine power at the top of the hill: your horse's hindlegs must be coming through well under his body if he is to jump properly. When coming up the hill you

Jumping from dark into light, or the other way round, requires a positive approach from the rider.

will need to aim for a point which gives you maximum space to straighten up and prepare for the fence.

The course now goes along the top of the hill, negotiating a hollow fence of small post-and-rail uprights in and out with a ditch in between. The lie of the land means that your horse will not see the ditch until he is about to jump the post-and-rail fence in, so you must be ready to ride positively in case he tries to stop. Do not look down at the ditch yourself or you will land in it!

A couple of easier fences – a woodpile and a stone wall – now follow before the next problem of a 'playpen'. There are various routes through this, with the most direct being over a large corner. If you attempt this route you will have to be sure that your steering is spot on, that your horse can jump corners (the middle of a competition is not the time to try one for the first time) and that you know exactly what you are doing and where you are aiming.

The alternatives to the corner are a bounce and a one-stride double. When faced with these choices, what you must know is the distances, so that you can decide which is the best route to tackle with your particular horse. You might find that the distance for the one-stride double is a little short: could you hold your horse and get a shorter stride in the middle, or are you likely to panic, drop the contact and cause a refusal? Sometimes the distance will be right providing you jump at a very precise spot – find a suitable landmark to give you an accurate point at which to aim, and ensure that you meet the fence at precisely the correct place.

A couple of straightforward fences follow before the next question, which asks the horse to jump over a small palisade into a wood. Many horses do not like jumping from light into dark, so positive signals from you will be needed. Beware of tipping forward as you approach the fence, as you will add to the weight on the horse's forehand, will have put yourself in a less effective position from which to drive him forward and, should he stop suddenly, or jump and peck on landing, you are likely to go over his head.

As the course now winds its way through the wood it is essential that you are able to steer and control the pace. Your schooling will pay dividends now, as the horse needs to be supple and obedient.

A short uphill canter brings you to a log on top of the hill and the land drops away on the landing side. You need plenty of impulsion as you come up the hill but must have a controlled, bouncy canter in order to negotiate the log without taking a flyer at it and landing in

COURSE WALK SUMMARY

■ Make sure you check the course plan before setting off on your course walk.

■ Walk the course several times if necessary, so that you know exactly where you are going.

■ As you walk, take account of the undulations of the ground and the siting of the fences.

■ Bear in mind the position of the previous fence and the one following as you walk the course.

■ If there are several options, check them all. Decide which one you will take, but have a secondary route in mind in case something goes amiss

with your first choice.

■ Do not assume that all take-offs and landings are safe: check them out, wading into water to discover what the landing is like.

■ Select a route that is best suited to your particular horse.

■ Take note of the ground conditions between fences, as there may be particularly hard or stony areas which are best avoided.

■ While there are advantages in walking a course with a knowledgeable friend, *you* must make the final decision on how you tackle a fence on your horse.

a heap. As there is a drop on the landing side, you must not be in a forward position or you will be likely to hit the deck.

The last fence is in sight – beware 'last fence-itis'. You cannot stop riding until you have crossed the finishing line, and even then you must still keep your horse balanced and together, easing him down gently from his canter to a walk. It is

ACTION POINTS

■ Ensure that your tack is in good condition and fits your horse well.

■ Protect yourself with a suitable crash hat and a body protector.

■ Make sure that both you and your

horse are fit enough for the task in hand.

■ Check that you can control your horse in open country – you may need to swap to a different bit or add a martingale.

An accident can easily happen, so wear a body protector and an approved hat when practising at home or schooling at a course, as well as in competitions.

tempting to see the last fence and think 'great, we're home', but this often results in poor riding: ride each fence to the best of your ability.

Judging pace

Hunter trials and cross country events are judged according to various criteria and you will need to check in the schedule for your particular event as to which are being applied. Obviously a clear round is required, but some events time the course from start to finish, others have a timed section (often within the course, but I have attended an event where those with clear rounds immediately went to a separate area to jump a timed section), while others have an optimum time and the person closest to this is the winner.

If you are doing a cross country course as part of a horse trials, where dressage, showjumping and cross country marks are added together to give a final score, the speed for the cross country should be given in the schedule.

SUMMARY

■ Go with your instructor to different cross country courses (most places are available for hire) so that you have experience of riding the different types of fences.

■ Walk the course very carefully – more than once is a good idea.

■ Remember that your horse has not seen the course – he is relying upon you for precise instructions.

TEN

Endurance Riding

Throughout history the horse has been involved in tremendous feats of endurance with, and for, man. Countless horses have carried men to war, undertaken tremendous journeys of exploration, assisted people to communicate with each other, travelled miles to further man's trade – pulling chariots or wagons, under saddle or acting as pack animals. When armies had to cover huge distances, there were guidelines as to how much the horses should carry and how fast they should travel – which are not that far divorced from the rules of the sport we know as endurance riding.

Endurance horses are superb equine athletes. They cover all kinds of terrain in varying weather conditions, with the prize at the end of it all being basically the rider's satisfaction in producing a horse at peak fitness who can complete a ride in good condition. Unlike the other equestrian sports, there are no large money prizes in top-level endurance riding, no indoor schools in which to compete, set courses over good going, or marks for conformation and turnout. The endurance horse's territory is the countryside itself, for the partnership of horse and rider have to negotiate fells, rivers, mountains, bridges, roads, hillside tracks – whatever lies in their way.

The challenge is to complete a certain distance within a designated time limit, with the horse finishing in a fit condition. These distances may range from pleasure rides of 24km (15 miles) or so, through competitive rides from 40km (25 miles) up to 64–80km (40–50 miles), and leading on to the ultimate challenges of the true endurance rides, such as those covering 160km (100 miles) in 24 hours. Some rides are spread over two or three days and the partnership must be fit enough to complete, say, 80km (50 miles) and then come out and cover a similar mileage on the next day.

THE ENDURANCE HORSE

All types of horses and ponies can be found competing in endurance riding, as it is a sport which anyone can enjoy. Some unlikely breeds have pursued long and successful careers, as their riders have tailored their competition demands to suit the horses' individual talents. Certainly at the lower levels you will not need a 'specialist' horse, as you would for eventing, for example. However, if you become hooked on the sport and have set your sights on the top-level rides, then certain types of horse are more suitable (like the Arabian); the most successful

You may be required to cross a stream or river on a long distance ride, so accustom your horse to water to enable him to be confident about going in and out.

usually being strong, compact, tough individuals.

As in any equestrian discipline, the endurance horse needs to have good conformation. If he is to travel efficiently over all kinds of terrain, he should not have any serious faults in this department, for the way in which the horse moves will be affected by his conformation. Horses with leg problems should definitely be avoided, as the mileage undertaken in training and competition will simply highlight any weaknesses. Special attention should also be given to the horse's feet, for the same reason.

Another important consideration for an endurance horse is temperament, as those who are constantly fizzed up will waste considerable amounts of energy (lazy types will waste considerable amounts of their rider's). While the good endurance animal is prepared to give a great deal more than is asked of him, he must also accept the rider's wishes without major arguments – another waste of physical and mental energy for both horse and rider. Endurance horses will need to take travelling and staying in strange stables in their stride, so the horse who will not eat and frets when away from home is not a good prospect.

Finally, horse and rider should enjoy each other's company. You will spend a

PREPARATION IS PARAMOUNT

Irrespective of breeding, conformation and temperament, no horse will be able to give of its best unless it is properly prepared.

great deal of time in training your horse for endurance rides, and if you really do not like him this is a recipe for disaster!

BENEFITS OF COMPETING

Endurance competitors are usually extremely friendly and willing to help newcomers – a terrific benefit in a sport from which you will learn a great deal about fitness and after-ride care. In fact, endurance riders have led the way in many areas of horse care: for example, the traditional teaching is to withhold food and water from a horse before and during competition, but for years long-distance competitors have demonstrated that this is unnecessary. They have also been effectively cooling off horses using methods – such as simply pouring cold water over the animal – which traditionalist teaching would have condemned, but which modern research at the highest level has shown to be the most beneficial for the horse. The open-mindedness of the endurance world has reaped many benefits for the welfare of horses, so if you are keen to be at the forefront of equine knowledge, the sport of long-distance riding is a good place to start.

Apart from the benefits of learning so much more about the horse's physiology, and the tremendous partnership which will develop between you and your horse, the rides are also held in some wonderful areas. In the UK, for example, the venues for rides can be as different as the Cumbrian Lakes and the fens of East Anglia, or the Welsh mountains and rolling downland. Endurance is also an international sport, with competitions held in Europe, Australia and the United States, a well as other countries. Some of

Washing down horses after a cross country schooling session – practical horse-care methods such as this have been pioneered in the endurance riding world. Your washing-down kit should include water, buckets, sponges, a sweat scraper and suitable rugs.

these rides, such as the Tevis Cup in the United States and the Quilty in Australia, are renowned throughout the world.

GETTING STARTED

In order to appreciate what is involved in endurance riding, the best idea is to visit some of the rides as a spectator. Contact the relevant organization for a list of rides at varying levels, held at a range of venues in different areas (see Useful Addresses).

When I first witnessed the sport back in the early 1980s I was amazed: firstly, at how quickly the horses covered the distance, and secondly, at the ease with which they tackled terrain which I would have thought twice about! Once you start competing you will realize just how clever and tough horses actually are, and how little we stimulate them with 'ordinary hacking'.

The other aspect which comes across strongly from visiting an endurance ride is the level of veterinary care involved. In many other sports, and particularly at the lower levels, riders can easily push their horses too far and too quickly – at local hunter trials I have witnessed three horses die because the riders had not paid sufficient attention to the animals' fitness preparation, or to how the horses were feeling on the day. However, in endurance the horse's welfare is carefully monitored before, during and after the competition. In some of the higher-level endurance rides horses and riders may be involved in a racing finish, but getting past the finishing post is only one obstacle as the most important hurdle is yet to come: the final vetting.

The rider's judgement therefore has a vital part to play throughout an endurance ride. By attending some rides as a spectator you will pick up tips on care, get an idea of the procedures involved (such as trotting up the horse for the vet), gain an insight into the phases of a ride and see the types of horse competing and their condition. To many ordinary riders the top-level endurance horse can appear rather lean, but on close inspection you will see that he is fit and well muscled rather than in poor condition. Carrying excess weight is not healthy for any horse, but when the animal is expected to travel over long distances it is even more unwise for him to be placing extra strain on his heart, lungs and limbs through being overweight.

Another useful way of gaining a good insight into a ride is to 'crew' for one of the competitors. For the longer rides, competitors meet their crew at various points in order to refresh horse and rider, while at certain mandatory halts the crew can take over the horse's care while the rider has a well-deserved rest.

TAKING PART

Most fit, sound horses can complete a pleasure ride without a great deal of extra preparatory work. However, for the higher mileages a more structured training programme will be needed (see Chapter 4). If endurance riding appeals to you, have a go at the pleasure rides, and from these you will be able to make fresh contacts who can offer advice on the next stage.

When preparing for and competing in endurance rides, it is worth taking note of the following:

MAP HOLDERS

Waterproof map holders, with cords attached so that you can hang the holder around your neck, are ideal. These can be purchased from any outdoor pursuit or camping shop.

- Make sure that your tack fits well and is clean and supple. Check the fitting of your saddle regularly, as your horse will change shape as he becomes fitter.
- In some rides it is permissible to equip your horse with protective boots, so check with the relevant society when entering the ride.
- Learn to read maps, and then practise reading them while on horseback. Although routes are marked, it is not unknown for some bright spark to remove a marker or alter its direction, so check your route regularly against the map when riding.
- Ensure that your horse is ridden on his own and in company during his preparation for long-distance rides.
- During competitions, do not just 'latch on' to another horse and rider – they may prefer to travel on their own.

TIP

One piece of equipment you should purchase at an early stage is a stethoscope (I bought mine via my vet). It will not only be invaluable on competitive rides, but will also be a useful addition to your first aid kit.

Hacking out in different areas will add variety and relaxation to your horse's fitness programme.

Riding out with a friend is helpful if you need to build your horse's confidence and overcome fear when encountering new sights and situations.

ACTION POINTS

■ Contact the endurance societies for details of their ride programmes.

■ Watch several rides, at all stages, to give you a clear picture of exactly what is involved..

- Make sure that you can control your horse at all paces, and always show consideration for other horses and riders.
- Rides will involve some work on roads, so do make sure your horse is well behaved in traffic.
- Keep the slogan 'to complete is to win' in mind and ensure that your horse's welfare is always the first priority.
- Once you start competing in rides where vet checks are compulsory, ensure that you can trot your horse up properly, with the horse moving actively and you allowing him enough freedom of his head and neck, and running alongside (not in front, which would block the vet's view).
- Make sure you are at your vet check at the appointed time.
- When passing through checkpoints, make sure that the steward has your number.
- Remember to thank all the officials and helpers who make each ride possible.
- Keep a training log of your horse's preparation and his competitive performances. This is useful for future reference and allows you to see where to improve your system or to pinpoint areas which need more work.
- Do not overdo the training, especially in the last few days before a ride.

TACK

There is no need to invest in any specialized tack when you first take part in endurance riding. Provided your horse's tack fits him well, you can enjoy the sport at the lower levels without any extra expense.

If you decide to pursue endurance riding more seriously, you may wish to invest in other equipment. For example, there are special saddles designed for endurance, as well as synthetic breastplates and martingales, and bridles which can be converted into headcollars in seconds. Some endurance riders like to use Western saddles – the choice is yours.

SUMMARY

■ All horses can enjoy some level of endurance riding, providing they are properly prepared.

■ A great deal can be learnt about fittening, feeding and caring for horses through taking part in endurance riding.

■ Some of the most beautiful parts of the country can become your riding territory.

ELEVEN

Competition Days

Careful preparation and attention to detail will make for a more successful competition day. If you know that your homework has been done, you have allowed enough time for all the jobs you have to do and you have everything you could need, you can relax and enjoy the day!

As you will have realized from reading the preceding chapters, preparation for a competition starts long before the day itself. Refining your and your horse's skills takes up by far the largest chunk of time, but once you are ready to compete you can use the schedule below to plan your preparations and make sure you do not forget anything vital.

SEVERAL WEEKS BEFORE

- Check out competition dates in magazines, local saddleries and feed merchants so that you know what is happening when.
- Send for the schedules and select your venues and classes.
- Send off your entries, if pre-entries are required. (If you have entered a show and your horse is then ill, ask your vet to provide a veterinary certificate. Most show organizers will reimburse your entry fees on production of the certificate.)

- Check that you have all you need for your classes, such as the correct dressage sheets or any extra tack.
- Work out when your farrier is due and how this relates to your competition date – you do not want a last-minute panic the night before the event because your horse has a loose or thin shoe.
- Check that your lorry tax, plating and insurance are up to date.
- Consider your horse's work programme in the lead-up to the competition: is there any extra schooling or fittening you want to incorporate?

TWO WEEKS BEFORE

- Start to learn your dressage tests/work out your individual show and practise elements of these as part of your normal schooling programme.
- Start to trim up your horse if necessary.
- If you are unsure of how to get to the venue or how long the trip will take, find time to do a 'dummy' run. Go in your car and then adjust the time taken according to your horse transport: doubling the time it takes in the car should give you plenty of time for travelling by lorry or with a trailer.

- If you have to call the event secretary for your times – for example, if you are entering a dressage competition, one-day event or endurance ride – make a note in your diary of when and whom to call.

THE DAY BEFORE

- Check your horse over – if he is lame, there is no need to go into the rest of this list!
- Clean your tack thoroughly.
- Ensure that all the horse's other equipment (travelling gear, protective boots, surcingle and so on) is clean and ready to use.
- Gather together everything you will need (see pages 150–151) and keep it in a handy place so that you can load your car or lorry efficiently.
- Prepare any haynets or feeds that you plan to take with you – large supplement containers with lids are useful for transporting feed.
- Work out your time schedule.
- Telephone the event secretary for your times, if applicable.
- Walk the course, if applicable (most cross country courses are open for spectators and competitors to walk the day before).
- Gather together all your riding gear and clean your boots.
- Check that your trailer or lorry is fully operational. Ensure that you have enough petrol or diesel and that the spare wheel is in good repair, and check the water and oil levels in your vehicle.
- Check that you have your breakdown service number handy in the car or lorry.
- Plait up your horse if necessary.

- If you use studs in your horse's shoes (see page 152), clean out and plug the stud holes.

WORKING OUT A TIME SCHEDULE

Working out a time schedule for the day of a competition ensures that you do all the jobs that are needed and gives you a time framework for your day, so that you know at a glance whether or not you are on schedule.

To work out your schedule, first list everything you have to do and then work out how long each of the jobs will take. Below is an example of such a schedule.

Task	Time (minutes)
Get up, wash and dress	20
Have breakfast	10
Load car	15
Travel to yard	15
Check and feed horse	5
Muck out and bed-down stable	15
Transfer equipment from car into lorry	15
Fill water container and load into lorry	5
Prepare lorry for horse to be loaded	5
Groom horse, check if sound	15
Prepare horse for travel	10
Load horse	5
Last-minute loading and checks	5
	140

From this sample schedule you can see that 2 hours 20 mins of the day have already gone – and you are only just ready to set off! Now you need to look at the time you need to be in action at the event, how long it will take for you to get there, how long you will need for warming up and so on.

Task	Time (minutes)
Journey	45
Collect number, locate arenas, unload, check horse, tack up	60
Warming up	40
Possible emergencies (eg delays on journey)	30
	175

This block of time totals 2 hours 55 minutes. Add this to the first block and you have 5 hours 15 minutes of effort before you even go into the ring – this means that to compete at, say, 9.40am you will have to get up at 4.25am. This is not at all unusual: in fact, the above example is a real schedule, albeit for an owner who often has to cope with her horse alone – and this particular horse loads easily!

If you work out this type of schedule before you even enter for a class (most schedules give approximate start times for their classes, or these can be worked out as you will always be told when the first class starts), then you will know whether perhaps you should ask the secretary for a later start time. Such a request is not too difficult to deal with for a dressage test, one-day event or endurance ride, as start times will be decided by the organizers. However, if you are showjumping there are no set times for competitors and it is up to you

to decide whether it is worth arriving later and possibly running the risk of missing your class.

Once you have all your times worked out, write down your schedule to keep you and your assistant (if any) on line for the day.

ON THE DAY

- Work to your time schedule, so that you know exactly how the day is going.
- If you plan to wear your jodhpurs to travel in, put on full-length chaps or tracksuit bottoms over the top to keep them clean.
- At the stables, feed and hay your horse and leave him in peace to eat his breakfast while you sort out the transport and load your equipment. Use your checklists to ensure that everything that is needed has been loaded. Muck out and prepare everything for your return.
- Lead out your horse and check that he is sound. It is far better to find out now if there is a problem than to go to the trouble of travelling all the way to the event.
- Assuming that all is well, groom your horse and prepare him for travel.
- Load the last-minute items such as your grooming kit and carry out one last check of your equipment list before you load the horse and set off.
- On arrival at the venue, check your horse and leave someone with the lorry or trailer while you find out where the competition rings are and locate the secretary's tent, toilets and so on.
- Check at the ringside which class is in progress so that you can decide on your next move.

Use a stocking to keep your horse's tail clean while travelling to a show. The tail bandage and tail guard are applied over the stocking.

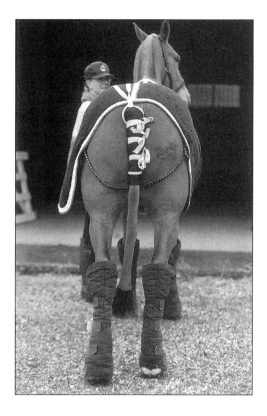

- Collect your number from the secretary.
- Unload your horse at a suitable time, take off his travelling gear and check him over. Brush him off and remove any stains he might have sustained while travelling.
- Fit studs, if used.
- Set out any equipment you will need on your return to the lorry, such as washing-down gear if you are competing cross country or in an endurance ride.
- Tack up your horse and ride him around to give him a chance to take in his surroundings.
- Allow enough time for you to change into your competitive gear before you warm up for your class.
- Check your girth a few minutes before you enter the ring.
- Now try to focus your attention on the job in hand. All your efforts over the past weeks or months have led to this moment, so do make the best of yourself and your horse.
- Above all, enjoy yourself.

INVALUABLE ASSISTANCE

■ If you have an assistant, s/he can put your number down on the board and keep you in touch with how many riders there are before you, when you need to make your way to the ring entrance, and so on.

■ Your assistant should carry a 'last-minute kit' consisting of a damp sponge to wipe off any foam around the horse's mouth or bit, a cloth to wipe over your boots, tack wipes to run over the tack (especially if you are entering in a showing class), a body brush to flick over the horse, a stable rubber to go over the horse's coat at the last minute, and hoof oil and brush so that you can oil the horse's hooves. All this can be carried in a bucket.

■ Your assistant can also take care of any rugs. If your start time is delayed and you need to keep moving, it is as well to pop a day rug over the horse's quarters if the weather is cold.

■ Your assistant can also remove brushing boots before you go in for a dressage test and take care of your schooling whip.

Post-competition care

- One-day events, which require you to complete three phases, will give your start times for all the disciplines. The amount of time you have available will determine whether or not you untack the horse in between phases, give it a small haynet, and so on.

- When waiting between classes or phases, make sure your horse is as comfortable as possible. At the very least, loosen the girth, loosen or undo the noseband (if you undo the lower straps of a flash noseband, tuck them into the cavesson section to prevent the horse chewing them), and keep him warm and dry.

- If you leave the horse tacked up in the lorry or trailer, remember your safety points: run up the stirrups and make them secure so that they cannot slip down, thread the reins through the throatlash, and do not leave the horse unattended.

- Do not leave your horse tied to the outside of the lorry or trailer without supervision at any time. It is very easy for a horse to become untied, get his leg over his leadrope, or be frightened by someone or something passing by, and this is when accidents happen.

- If your horse has finished his competitive day, attend to his immediate needs. For example, if he has just finished his cross country round he may need to be washed off (or properly cooled down if the weather is very hot) and then led around until his breathing has returned to normal (see page 59).

- Check your horse over for any cuts, signs of heat and so on. If you locate a problem, treat as necessary.

- Rug up the horse as required and then let him drink and eat a feed or have a haynet.

- If the horse is eating a feed, let him do so in peace – you can always occupy yourself by wiping over the tack,

At shows, keep an eye on your horse while he is tied up to the lorry. It can take only a second for him to injure himself, and if he indulges in vices like wood chewing you need to be there to discourage him, or your lorry will be damaged and the horse could also create problems for himself.

loading equipment into the lorry or trailer and preparing the vehicle for the horse to be loaded.

- Prepare the horse for travel and then load him.
- Pack away anything left outside the lorry or trailer.
- Return your number to the secretary and collect your dressage sheet, if applicable. If the results of your class are available, check how you fared (and collect any rosette or winnings!). Before you leave, thank the secretary – many people give up their free time to organize shows and other events, so a few appreciative words from the competitors will be welcome.
- Before you set off, carry out a last-minute check around your area. It should be as you found it (do not muck out your lorry or trailer into the field) and check that your horse is still okay.
- Perhaps you want to have a look at some classes before leaving the showground? Fine – but *always* attend to your horse's needs *first*.

On the way home

- You will probably be reflecting on how the day went and where you could improve for next time. Even if you have had a bad day, there is probably something for you to learn, which is a positive outcome.
- You may be tired and keen to get home, but do drive considerately.
- When you arrive home, do include mucking out the lorry on your list of jobs.

Later in the day

- Try to make a late check on your

horse to ensure that he is eating well and that there are no signs of trouble brewing, such as heat or swelling in his legs.
- Clean your tack: the job gets more unattractive the longer you leave it!

THE NEXT DAY

- Check over your horse thoroughly.
- Depending on how strenuous the competition was, you may want to give your horse a day off. If you do work him, give him a light day, perhaps taking him for a hack to let him stretch his legs rather than asking him to do any demanding school work.
- Make sure that your horse has some time out at liberty in the field.
- Depending on how you and your horse performed at the event, start planning for your next outing, working in extra sessions as required.

EQUIPMENT CHECKLISTS

Dressage

Horse

- Saddle, complete with numnah or saddle cloth if used, leathers, irons and girth
- Breastplate, if used
- Bridle with snaffle bit, or double bridle if applicable. You may wish to use rubber-backed reins for extra grip in hot or rainy conditions. Check that the noseband you are using is allowed
- Brushing boots, if used. These are for working in only, so ask your helper to remove them before you enter the arena for your test
- Dressage test and rule book

Rider

- Approved riding hat
- Jacket
- Breeches
- Long boots
- Gloves
- Stock and pin or collar and tie
- Whip
- Spurs (where these are permitted)

Showjumping

Horse

- Jumping saddle, complete with numnah or saddle cloth if used, leathers, irons and girth
- Surcingle
- Bridle with rubber reins
- Running martingale if required, plus stops to prevent the martingale rings getting caught up on the rein buckles. If a breastplate is worn, a running martingale attachment can be used
- Protective boots – tendon, brushing or overreach – as required
- Studs in shoes and stud kit

Rider

As for dressage (above).

Cross country

Horse

- Saddle, with numnah or saddle cloth if used, leathers, irons and girth
- Breastplate (advisable)
- Surcingle
- Bridle – you may need to use a stronger bit than normal. Your reins should be long enough for you to knot them at the end, and rubber reins are better for grip
- Protective boots, or bandages plus suitable padding, needle and thread, and insulating tape
- Grease for horse's legs

Rider

- As for dressage, but with a coloured top in place of your jacket and a coloured silk on top of a jockey skull cap
- Body protector

Showing

Horse

- Saddle and bridle as appropriate to the particular class (see Chapter 6)

Rider

As for dressage, but the type of jacket depends on the particular class.

Endurance

Horse

No special tack is required, but it must be a good fit.

Rider

- Suitable riding hat and footwear
- Other clothing as applicable to weather conditions. There are no strict rules

Washing-down equipment

- Water in a large container
- Buckets
- Sponges
- Towels
- Sweat scraper
- Wicking-type rug, or sweat sheet and summer sheet, together with roller or elasticated surcingle to secure if the summer sheet does not have cross surcingles

First aid kit

You should carry a small first aid kit for horse and rider with you in your lorry or trailer.

USING STUDS

In order to give your horse better grip and a firmer footing when jumping at speed or turning, studs can be used. These are screwed into his shoes for the duration of the jumping round and are then removed. Some studs are kept in the shoes permanently: for instance, your farrier may fit small road studs if your horse has to do a lot of work on slippery road surfaces.

Studs used in competition come in different styles, from long and pointed to square and chunky. They can be bought from saddlers, but you will need your farrier to put stud holes into your horse's shoes when he makes them. Some riders use just one stud per shoe, placed on the outside branch, but this does unbalance the horse's foot. Although studs are generally used in the hind shoes, some competitors do use them in the front as well.

When your farrier shoes your horse, you can plug the stud holes with cotton wool. This helps to keep the holes clean: it is a simple job to remove the wool plugs with a nail when you want to insert the studs. Once the plug has been removed, insert a stud tap into the hole to clear any debris. Remove the tap, and then screw in the stud and tighten using a spanner.

When using studs, take note of the following:

- Avoid taking your horse on roads or similar surfaces when he has studs in. If you were to do this, he would effectively be on stilts and the concussive effects along his limbs would be very detrimental.

- Studs can cause considerable damage if your horse treads on your foot, so do be careful.

- If you put your horse into your lorry or trailer when he is wearing studs it is sensible to have an additional layer, such as rubber matting, on the floor to prevent damage.

- Remember to plug the stud hole when not in use, and always use gloves to protect your hands when fitting or removing studs.

ACTION POINTS

- Visit events or shows as a spectator and watch how the most successful riders prepare and ride their horses, and then take care of them afterwards. You will pick up numerous useful tips.

- If you use studs, invest in some extra rubber matting for your lorry/trailer and ramp to use when your horse is in the vehicle between classes.

- If possible, enlist the help of a reliable assistant for competition days.

SUMMARY

- Forward planning is essential.

- Know the rules for your particular sport so that you are not caught out by any changes in requirements.

- Practise skills such as plaiting so that on competition morning you can work efficiently and save time.

- Always put your horse's needs first.

Useful Addresses

United Kingdom

British Horse Society
British Equestrian Centre
Stoneleigh
Warks CV8 2LR
The umbrella organization for groups covering the administration of a wide range of equestrian sports.

British Show Hack, Cob & Riding Horse Association
Chamberlain House
Chamberlain Walk
88 High Street
Coleshill
Nr Birmingham B46 3BZ

British Show Jumping Association
see British Horse Society

Dressage Group
see British Horse Society

Driving Group
see British Horse Society

Endurance Riding Group
see British Horse Society

Endurance Horse & Pony Society
Mr O. Hare
Mill House
Mill Lane
Stoke Bruerne
Northants NN12 7SH

Horse Trials Group
see British Horse Society

National Pony Society
Willingdon House
102 High Street
Alton
Hants GU34 1EN

Ponies (UK)
Chesham House
56 Green End Road
Sawtry
Huntingdon
Cambs PE17 5UY

Riding Clubs and The Pony Club
These two organizations have their headquarters at the British Equestrian Centre but operate branches and local clubs nationwide. The Pony Club is for young people aged up to 21 years; the Riding Clubs movement is for adult riders, although many clubs also have junior sections.

Side Saddle Association
Highbury House
19 High Street
Welford
Northampton NN6 6HT

Scottish Endurance Riding Club
9 Elliot Road
Jedburgh
Roxburgh TD8 6HN

Western Horseman's Association of Great Britain
13 East View
Barnet
Herts EN5 5TL

Breed Societies

Arab Horse Society
Windsor House
Ramsbury
Nr Marlborough
Wilts SN8 2PE

British Appaloosa Society
c/o 36 Clusterbolts
Stapleford
Herts SG14 3ND

British Palomino Society
Penrhiwllan
Llandysul
Dyfed SA44 5NZ

British Skewbald and Piebald Association
West Fen House
High Road
Little Downham
Ely
Cambs CB6 2TB

Coloured Horse & Pony Society (UK)
Pampard House
Bradden Lane
Gaddesden Row
Hemel Hempstead
Herts HP2 6JB

Connemara Pony Society
2 The Leys
Salaford
Chipping Norton
Oxon OX7 5FD

Dales Pony Society
196 Springvale Road
Walkley
Sheffield
S. Yorks S6 3NU

Dartmoor Pony Society
57 Pykes Down
Ivybridge
Devon PL21 0BY

Exmoor Pony Society
Glenfern
Waddicombe
Dulverton
Somerset TA22 9RY

Fell Pony Society
Riccarton Mill
Newcastleton
Roxburgh TD9 0SN

Highland Pony Society
Beechwood
Elie
Fife KY9 1DH

New Forest Pony & Cattle Breeding Society
Beacon Cottage
Burley
Ringwood
Hants BH24 4EW

Shetland Pony Stud Book Society
Pedigree House
6 Kings Place
Perth PH2 8AD

Welsh Part-bred Horse Group
Bromsden Farm Stud
Henley on Thames
Oxon RG9 4RG

Welsh Pony & Cob Society
6 Chalybeate Street
Aberystwyth
Dyfed SY23 1HS

United States of America

American Horse Council
1700 K Street NW
Suite 300
Washington
DC 20006

American Horse Shows Association
220 E 42nd Street
4th Floor
New York
NY 10017

International Side-saddle Organization
PO Box 282
Alton Bay
NH 03810

National 4-H Council
7100 Connecticut Avenue
Chevy Chase
MD 20815
For details of the 4-H Program (a youth organization). Alternatively, contact your local Cooperative Extension Agent.

US Pony Clubs Inc
The Kentucky Horse Park
4071 Iron Works Pike
Lexington
KY 40511

Breed Societies

American Morgan Horse Association
PO Box 960
3 Bostwick Road
Shelburne
VT 05482

American Quarter Horse Association
2701 I–40 East
Amarillo
TX 79168

American Saddlebred Horse Association
4093 Ironworks Pike
Lexington
KY 40511

Appaloosa Horse Club
PO Box 8304
Moscow
ID 83843

International Arabian Horse Association
PO Box 33696
Denver
CO 80233

American Hackney Horse Society
4059 Ironworks Pike
Building A
Lexington
KY 40511

American Shetland Pony Club
PO Box 3415
Peoria
IL 61612–3415

National Show Horse Registry
11700 Commonwealth Drive
Suite 200
Louisville
KY 40299

Paso Fino Horse Association
PO Box 600
100 W Main Street
Bowling Green
FL 33834

Welsh Pony and Cob Association of America
PO Box 2977
Winchester
VA 22601

Australia

EFA – Federal Body
52 Kensington Road
Rose Park
SA 5067
Administration only.

EFA – Northern Territory
PO Box 1244
Palmerston
MT 0831

EFA – NSW
GPO Box 4317
Sydney
NSW 2001

EFA – Queensland
PO Box 1417
Beeleigh
QLD 4207

EFA – South Australia
PO Box 1177
Marleston
SA 5033

EFA – Tasmania
PO Box 94
Glenorchy
TAS 7010

EFA – Victoria Royal Showgrounds
Epsom Road
Ascot Vale
VIC 3032

EFA – Western Australia
PO Box 376
Midland
WA 6056

The Hack Council of New South Wales
PO Box 61
East Gosford 2250

The Hack Council of Western Australia
9 Stevens Road
Bedfordale
WA 6112

Royal Show Societies NSW
Royal Agricultural Society of NSW
GPO Box 4317
Sydney
NSW 2001

Index